# About the Author

Philip Shallcrass (a.k.a. Greywolf) is a poet, writer, artist, musician, storyteller and has been a student and practitioner of Druidry since 1974. As founder and joint chief of the British Druid Order, he presents talks and workshops and represents Druidry at interfaith gatherings, academic conferences on contemporary religions and on television in the UK, Europe and the USA. As a Druid priest, he organises open celebrations of seasonal festivals at sacred sites, conducts rites of passage such as blessings for children, Druid weddings or handfastings and funerals, and offers counselling. As a composer and performer he promotes knowledge and practice of the bardic arts. He has written widely on Druidry and the bardic tradition as well as providing information to other writers and researchers. Philip lives in Sussex with his wife, Ellie, and two young children, Jo and Michael.

# Druidry

**Piatkus Guides**

*Other titles in this series include*

African Wisdom
Angels
Astrology
Celtic Wisdom
Colour Healing
Crystal Wisdom
Earth Mysteries
The Essential Nostradamus
Feng Shui
Kabbalah
Maya Prophecy
Meditation
Palmistry
Pendulum Dowsing
Psychic Awareness
Reiki
Shamanism
Tarot
Tibetan Buddhism

A PIATKUS GUIDE

# Druidry

*Philip Shallcrass*

**PIATKUS**

For my boys, Jo, Michael and Dickon,
and for all the women in my life,
but most especially
for Ellie, Bobcat and my mother.

© 2000 Philip Shallcrass

First published in 2000 by
Judy Piatkus (Publishers) Ltd
5 Windmill Street, London W1P 1HF

For the latest news and information
on all our titles visit our new website at
www.piatkus.co.uk

The moral rights of the author have been asserted

*A catalogue record for this book is available from the British Library*

ISBN 0-7499-2040-8

Typeset by Action Publishing Technology Limited, Gloucester
Printed and bound in Great Britain by
Mackays of Chatham PLC

# Contents

# Acknowledgements

I'm indebted to my guides and teachers and all my friends in the Druid community who have contributed to my understanding of our tradition. I'm especially grateful to Bobcat, through whose generosity of spirit I have learned more in the last five years than in the previous 20. Philip Carr-Gomm and Ronald Hutton have provided much of lasting value, not least, their friendship. I thank my children for their patience during my hours at the word processor. And, of course, I thank Ellie, whose unfailing support has given me the freedom to be who I am.

# Introduction

## Why Druidry?

Hail and welcome! You are about to enter a world in which people and animals talk to each other and take on each other's shapes, in which trees communicate through their own language, a language you can learn to speak and read. It is a world of visions, spirit guides, journeys into other worlds, ancestral teachers, past lives, and gods who are at once ancient and ever young; such is the world of the Druid.

The last decade has seen a growing interest in Druidry. Demand for books, talks and workshops on the subject has never been greater. Yet why should a philosophy rooted deep in the prehistoric past still have relevance in our technological age? What is it in the teachings of our ancestors that speaks to us across the centuries?

At the heart of Druidry is the quest for inspiration. We seek it in the beauty of the natural world, in relationships, in music, poetry and song, in dreams and visions, in active ritual or quiet contemplation and in the wisdom of our ancestors. Once our personal sources of inspiration have been found, we learn to work with them to awaken and sustain creativity, expressed through the arts and through how we live our lives and conduct our relationships. Inspiration manifests itself in healing on many levels and in increased awareness and understanding. Ultimately, it moves through creativity and knowledge and penetrates to the soul, where it transforms into magic and mystery. Personal growth is part of the process, but Druidry also works with and for communities, the wider world, and other worlds beyond.

Druidry offers reconnection and healing to all aspects of being. We reconnect with the natural world, the cycles of time, and the processes of change, birth, death and renewal by celebrating the seasons of the sun and the phases of the moon and by honouring and working with both the substance and the spirit of the mineral, plant and animal worlds. We reconnect with our families and friends by gathering together to celebrate festivals and the rites of passage that mark our personal growth and our changing relationships with those around us and with the world. We reconnect with our heritage by honouring our ancestors, their lives, teachings and beliefs; and with the land through meditation or through rituals at sacred places, whether they be trees, streams or the stone circles of our ancestors. Through reawakening these links, we become aware of who we are and our role in the great dance of creation.

Druidry offers an holistic approach to life, honouring and celebrating the physical as well as the spiritual. It is a green philosophy, a philosophy that affirms life, seeing all creation as sacred. It is an attitude of mind that fosters respect, understanding and love.

This book aims to serve as a guide to the Druid path, awakening the reader to the teachings of our ancestors, gods and guides, and to the spirits of the natural world, of sun, moon and stars, tree and leaf, wind and rain, sea and river, fur and feather. The reader will learn to find new and potent relationships with our ancestors of blood and spirit, to create and work within sacred space, to attune to the changing patterns of the natural world through celebration of its cycles, and to access and work with the flowing spirit of inspiration that we call Awen.

So, to return to the two questions asked at the beginning of this introduction: why should a philosophy rooted deep in the prehistoric past still have relevance in our technological age? What is it in the teachings of our ancestors that speaks to us across the centuries? The answer to both is that Druidry offers the tools we need to recreate our world by recreating ourselves.

## Dogmas and Catmas

There are no dogmas in Druidry, just 'catmas'. Dogmas are rigid beliefs, often received from others, that tend to stifle freedom of thought and expression. Catmas are fluid beliefs, held only as long as they have value, perhaps until they are superseded by our growth in experience and understanding. Catmas offer us the freedom to behave *as if* our beliefs are true, allowing us to thoroughly test their worth. For example, one of my catmas is that spirits of nature are as real as the computer on which I'm writing these words, enabling me to interact with them with respect. A few years ago I believed differently, however. And in a few years' time my opinion may change again. You may believe that such spirits are poetic metaphors or psychological projections. That's fine. All I ask is that you allow yourself the freedom to try out the belief systems in this book and see if they work for you. So, before we begin, let your dogmas off their leashes and allow them to run free. They may race around in chaotic confusion for a while, but give them time and you will find that, one by one, they turn into self-reliant, cool catmas.

## Dates

The dating in this book replaces the Christian system of BC and AD – Before Christ and Anno Domini (Year of Our Lord) – with the culturally broader BCE and CE – Before the Common Era and in the Common Era. This system is used increasingly by students of comparative religion, non-European cultures, history and prehistory who see it as more inclusive of the many beliefs that make up the rich diversity of human experience than the purely Christian BC/AD system of dating.

## Sex

I don't use the word Druidess – a Druid is a Druid whether male or female. To avoid endless repetition of terms such as 'she or he' or clumsy modernisms such as 's/he', I have alternated more or less randomly between he and she. I use the plural 'gods' to mean both male gods and female goddesses, while using god and goddess for individual deities as appropriate.

# Part I

# The Circle is Unbroken

# 1

# Beginnings

As a child I used to stare into mirrors. If I stared long enough my face would fade away to be replaced by that of an old man with a bald head and a wispy, white beard. His eyes were white as though he were blind, yet I felt that he looked from the mirror into the innermost recesses of my soul. I didn't know who he was, but I looked forward to those encounters, knowing that the old man's presence would always lead me to look deep inside myself and strive towards the realisation of my deepest dreams. It took me years to realise that he was the perfect representation of my idea of the archetypal Druid, and that he was my guide, the silent, knowing teacher of my heart, mind and spirit.

When thinking of a Druid, most people probably conjure up a similar picture – an old man with a white beard and robe to match, perhaps armed with a staff and an enigmatic smile, an age-old wisdom in his ageless eyes. This is the Druid archetype we have inherited, filtered to us through myth and fiction as Merlin, Gandalf and Getafix. But where does the archetype come from, how close is it to the reality of Druidry, either as it is now or as it was in the past, and what can we learn from it?

Look inside yourself. What is *your* image of the archetypal Druid? Is he an ancient, white-bearded sage? Is he a wild shaman dressed in animal skins and feathers? Is your Druid a woman? Find the image and hold it in your mind. What does it tell you about your own yearnings, beliefs and aspirations? What does it say to you? Does your Druid have a name, a background, a history, a message or a lesson for you? Spend some time in the company of your Druid archetype, then, when you are ready to continue, give thanks for what you have seen, felt and learned.

Aware of your own image of the Druid, let us now look at other images of Druidry, both past and present.

## Honouring Our Ancestors

One of the things that attracts people to Druidry is the sense that it provides a link with the past. For the Druid, the past is not a static thing held fast within the dry and dusty pages of history books, but a living part of our reality; it is how we became who we are and the blueprint for what we may yet become. The past is a potent source of inspiration. More than that, the past is the realm of our ancestors and, for the Druid, our ancestors are our companions and teachers in this life.

We speak of our ancestors of blood and of spirit. Those of blood are our genetic line – our parents, grandparents, great-grandparents, back 10,000 years to the time after the last Ice Age when people first walked the land of Britain, back three million years to when the first humans walked the plains of Southern Africa, back further to the single-celled life forms of three billion years ago. The earth on which we walk and the sedimentary rocks below are the remains of our ancestors in this chain of evolution. We honour this chain of other lives that have given us the life we have now. To remind ourselves of the connection between the earth and our ancestors, we sometimes chant to the rhythm of a drum: 'Earth and stone, blood and bone, all are one, all are one.'

In working with our ancestors, we begin by honouring our parents. Many of us find our own parents harder to relate to than an ancestor who lived a thousand years ago or more; we are too close. But whatever problems we may have had in childhood, we give thanks to our parents for the extraordinary gift of life.

We also recognise that difficult experiences contribute strongly to who we are. Perhaps arguing against your parents has helped to form your strength of character, hone your mind and increase your independence. Perhaps their behaviour towards you has helped you to form strong relationships with others. Perhaps the absence of one or both parents has helped you to become self-reliant. Positive results often come from negative experiences. Look for those things of value that you have learned from your parents and give thanks. The healing process has begun ...

We honour our grandparents, our great-grandparents and their forebears through the generations in the same way, giving thanks for the gift of life passed down the chain of DNA and for the lessons learned or the cultural, physical and spiritual inheritance gained from them.

We also honour our ancestors of spirit, those who have walked paths similar to our own in previous generations. Some may belong to our blood line, others may be unrelated in any direct genetic sense but will have world views, beliefs and experiences that link us to them in spirit. Those who follow the Druid path look to these spiritual ancestors as teachers and guides. We give thanks for what we have gained from them.

Let's walk back now along the path of the Druid tradition and see who we encounter and what we may learn from them, and they from us.

## Druids Today

The Druid of today may be the most difficult to envisage. There is such great diversity among modern Druids, who express a wide range of beliefs through many different practices. Certain groups focus on the spiritual, others on cultural or social activities, politics and protest, while some combine all of these things. Modern Druidry is represented by equal numbers of women and men from a wide range of backgrounds.

Some wear robes when taking part in group ritual. These come in a variety of colours and styles, though white or natural unbleached fibres are the most common. Just as many, perhaps more, don't even own a robe. With such diversity, it may seem hard to find a common thread, yet all are responding to their own vision of the Druid archetype.

When exploring Druidry, many find group rituals helpful; it offers a real sense of kinship and community. Those attending their first Druid ceremony often describe a feeling of homecoming. Most Druid rites are small, perhaps a few friends gathered round a fire in a forest at twilight making offerings of bread and mead to the ancestors, sharing food and laughter, along with stories and songs, teaching and ritual. After a few hours they will leave, tired but elated, waking the next day refreshed in spirit for the tasks ahead. By contrast, open rites held at festivals at major sacred sites may attract hundreds. Such rites, whether on a small or large scale, form only a small part of the life of the modern Druid. She will practise her craft in many other ways, as a healer, counsellor, teacher, artist, writer, poet or parent, each activity informed and underpinned by the understanding that comes through Druidry.

## The Altar

In her home, the Druid will often have an altar on which will be arranged a collection of things reflecting her personal and ancestral history, her interests and beliefs. There may be figures of gods, perhaps of her own land, perhaps from other cultures with which she has a strong spiritual link. The altar is a place to commune with the spirits of nature, so there will usually be elements of the natural world: feathers, leaves, bones, stones, nuts, perhaps a bowl of earth or sand and another of water. There will often be an incense burner, incense, herbs and candles. There may be gifts or tokens from friends or mementoes of her family, pictures of children, lovers, parents, grandparents. The common link connecting all these things and the reason for their presence on the altar is that they provide inspiration.

If you don't have an altar, you might like to make one. Clear a space on a shelf, in a corner or on a table and think about what you will place there. What do you have already that you find inspiration in? Perhaps a painting that would make a good backdrop, perhaps a stone from a place sacred to our ancestors or special to you. Gather a few things together and see how they fit. Think about what each one means to you and why. Your altar is a reflection of yourself. What do the things you put on it say about who you are and who you would like to be? Aim to make your altar reflect the very best of yourself and your aspirations. Remember that your altar doesn't have to stay the same any more than you do. If some things that you place there lose or change their meaning, put them away and replace them with things that more accurately reflect your growing awareness.

The altar is a daily reminder of the spiritual dimension in our lives, a focus for meditation and prayer, a place to make offerings to our ancestors and gods. These offerings may be of thought or word, of poetry or song, of incense, oil or water, of food or flowers. Offerings are what we give of ourselves in return for the blessings we are given of life, of teaching, of healing and wisdom.

Now, from the present day and the secure foundation of the altar, let us journey into the past. As we travel, look for those aspects of Druid history that inspire you most. What follows is a necessarily short and selective history. If you want to know more, you'll find a list of recommended further reading at the back of this book.

## Druid Revivals

In 1964 Ross Nichols founded the Order of Bards, Ovates and Druids (OBOD), his aim being to take Druidry back to what he saw as its Celtic roots. By the late 1970s Druidry was beginning to absorb elements of Wicca, the 'new' pagan religion constructed by Nichols' friend, Gerald Gardner. Druids were also beginning to be influenced by Siberian, Native American and other indigenous cultures, rediscovering through these the roots of native European tradition. Between them these influences, along with research into medieval manuscripts of Wales and Ireland, fuelled the re-creation of Druidry as a magical, holistic, earth-ancestor spirituality. My own group, the British Druid Order (BDO) emerged from this cauldron of ideas and inspiration.

Before the 1970s, the image of the Druid presented in the

popular press was of men in white robes standing in a circle at Stonehenge at the summer solstice. This annual spectacle was as much a part of the English summer as cricket and cream teas. It seemed that that was how it had always been: robed figures in the twilight before the dawn, performing elaborate rituals then disappearing again until the following summer.

Go back 100 years and that image changes again. The Druids of that time are most strongly represented in the public mind by the Welsh Gorsedd of Bards. The Gorsedd still appears in early August at the National Eisteddfod, the great annual celebration of Welsh language and culture. Their robes are one of three colours: blue for a bard, green for an ovate and white for a Druid, and they perform ornate ceremonies in modern stone circles built for the purpose in towns in which the Eisteddfod is held. They speak Welsh, calling for peace: '*Heddwch!*'; a sword is unsheathed and sheathed again to signify that peace does indeed exist. Young girls bring flowers to the central altar stone on which the Archdruid stands. The Hirlas Horn is passed around, and the bard who has composed the best poem in a traditional metre is presented with a chair.

Go back a little over 200 years and you reach the high point of the 18th-century Druid revival. It is the summer solstice of 1792 and we are atop Primrose Hill in London. There we find a small gathering led by a Welsh stonemason, failed businessman and literary forger called Edward Williams, also known by his bardic name, Iolo Morganwg. Standing in a circle of pebbles brought in his pockets, and dressed in the standard street clothes of his day, he makes the call for peace, unsheathes and sheaths a sword and declaims the Gorsedd Prayer:

*Grant, O God, thy protection,*
*and in protection, strength,*
*and in strength, understanding,*
*and in understanding, knowledge,*
*and in knowledge, the knowledge of justice,*
*and in the knowledge of justice, the love of it,*
*and in that love, the love of all existences,*
*and in the love of all existences, the love of God,*
*God and all goodness.*

This prayer is still heard at the Welsh National Eisteddfod every year. In various forms, it is also heard at the ceremonies of many other Druid groups, though many now replace the word 'God' with 'spirit' or 'spirits', 'gods' or 'goddess' or 'god and goddess'.

Iolo's Primrose Hill ceremony marked the formation of the Gorsedd of Bards of the Isle of Britain whose colourful ceremonies enhance the Eisteddfod. Iolo claimed to have found the rites and laws of the Gorsedd in ancient Welsh manuscripts and, for 150 years after his death, most people believed him. Then a scholar going through Iolo's papers found draft versions of the supposedly ancient manuscripts, all in Iolo's own handwriting; virtually the whole of Iolo's vast and complex system of bardic and Druidic lore was his own invention. Many now dismiss Iolo and his contemporaries as at best romantics, at worst frauds. However, when Iolo turned his hand to forging medieval Welsh poetry he was able to pass off his own verses as the work of Wales's greatest medieval bard, Dafydd ap Gwilym. In fact Iolo's fakes actually became more popular than Dafydd's originals. Iolo clearly had talent, even genius.

As a child, Iolo was inspired by his mother's tales of great days past, when every Welsh noble house had its household bard. Later, he found inspiration in visits to the great stone circles of Avebury and Stonehenge. His inspiration led directly to the foundation of the Welsh Gorsedd and all that it does to promote and preserve Welsh language and culture. He also inspired the foundation of the National Library of Wales and the University of Wales.

Iolo was responding to a popular fascination with Druidry that had begun in the 17th century. The antiquarian John Aubrey (1626–97) was the first to link Druids with prehistoric stone circles such as Stonehenge. He was followed by an eccentric Christian minister, William Stukeley (1687–1765), who, like Aubrey before him, visited Stonehenge and Avebury. Stukeley turned his garden into a Druid grove, filled his sermons with references to Druids and called himself, 'Chyndonax of Mount Haemus, Druid'. He considered Druidry to be a patriarchal religion, brought to Britain after the biblical Flood and portrayed Druids as proto-Christians, practising what he called Natural Religion. Stukeley's ideas were picked up by the visionary poet and artist, William Blake (1757–1827). Blake not only saw Druids as proto-Christians, he identified biblical figures such as Noah and Abraham as Druids.

William Wordsworth (1770–1850) and other poets of the period wrote of Druids, while contemporary artists, including two of England's finest, Turner and Constable, produced paintings and drawings of Stonehenge. Through their work, the image of the Druid returned into mainstream British culture.

## Druid Survivals

Bardic colleges existed in Scotland until the 18th century. A century before there had been similar institutions in Wales and Ireland. They represented a direct link with the Druidry of the remote past, when bards were members of the Druid class among the tribal peoples of Europe in the centuries before our Common Era. Trainees in the bardic colleges were expected to commit to memory great quantities of poetry, the lore and legends of their ancestors, and the genealogies of important families, just as their predecessors had done in the time of Julius Caesar.

Druids were advisers to Irish kings until at least the 10th century, whilst bards refer to Druids as active in Wales in the 12th century. This was the period when ancient tales of pagan gods and heroes were committed to writing in Britain and Ireland, often by Christian monks. In these stories, Druids are portrayed as royal counsellors, prophets, poets, magicians, healers and interpreters of dreams and omens, with the ability to divine and prophesy the future, raise magic mists, brew cauldrons with miraculous healing powers, raise the dead, alter the weather, change themselves and others into birds or animals and bring down tyrants with their curses. They were an altogether wilder and more magical breed than the Druid revivalists of the 18th century.

In the late medieval period many Druidic functions were attributed to Merlin in the tales of King Arthur and his knights. The character of Merlin we know now was created in the 12th century by Geoffrey of Monmouth, who drew on Welsh legends surrounding two bards of the so-called Dark Ages. The first, Myrddin Emrys, was portrayed as a prophet, magician and adviser to the 5th-century British king Ambrosius. The second, Myrddin Wyllt ('the Wild'), was a household bard in 6th-century Scotland. Seeing the lord of his household and all his companions killed in battle, he fled human company and lived in the wild Forest of Celydon with a wolf and a pig. He gained a reputation as an inspired prophet. Both Myrddins lived at a time when much of Europe, including Britain and Ireland, was in transition from paganism to Christianity, and they retain many of the qualities of pagan Druids.

## Classical Druids

Back another 500 years from the Dark Ages and you come to the beginning of the Common Era and the first written records of Druids. The few surviving descriptions of Druids given by Greek and Roman writers of the last few centuries BCE and the first few centuries CE were the inspiration behind the antiquarians of the 17th century who, in turn, inspired the 18th-century Druid revival. Among the most influential was the Greek historian Pliny the Elder. In a passage from his *Natural History*, written in the 1st century CE, he gives a vivid account of Druid beliefs and a rite held in a forest grove:

> The Druids ... held nothing more sacred than the mistletoe and the tree that bears it, always supposing that tree to be the oak. But they choose groves formed of oaks for the sake of the tree alone, and they never perform any of their rites except in the presence of a branch of it ... In fact they think that everything that grows on it has been sent from heaven and is a proof that the tree was chosen by the god himself. The mistletoe, however, is found but rarely upon the oak; and when found, is gathered with due religious ceremony, if possible on the sixth day of the moon (for it is by the moon that they measure their months and years, and also their ages of thirty years). They choose this day because the moon, though not yet in the middle of her course, has already considerable

influence. They call the mistletoe by a name meaning, in their language, the all-healing. Having made preparation for sacrifice and a banquet beneath the trees, they bring thither two white bulls, whose horns are bound then for the first time. Clad in a white robe, the priest ascends the tree and cuts the mistletoe with a golden sickle, and it is received by others in a white cloak. Then they kill the victims, praying that the god will render this gift of his propitious to those to whom he has granted it. They believe that the mistletoe, taken in drink, imparts fecundity to barren animals, and that it is an antidote for all poisons.

Pliny has his Druid dressed in white, while other contemporary writers refer to Druids dressed in red robes edged with gold and to women who were probably Druids wearing black robes.

Present-day Druids recognise aspects of Pliny's description as relevant to our practice: his presentation of Druidry as a magical belief system; his honouring of the passage of time and the cycles of nature through the phases of the moon; his concern with the healing properties of herbs and with the spirits resident in trees, plants and animals. Modern Druids don't sacrifice animals, though some may wonder why that is if we are seeking to revive an ancient tradition which animal sacrifice was a part of. The answer is that we are not trying to revive Druidry as it might have been 2,000 years ago. Those were harsher times, when food was scarce and death from famine, disease or warfare an ever-present threat. Life for most of us is very different now. Druidry is a living tradition. Just as times change and human consciousness evolves, so too Druidry changes and evolves, renewing its relevance for each new generation.

What else do we know about the ancient Druids? In the 1st century BCE, the Greek historian Diodorus Siculus gave the following account of the Druids of his day:

> And there are among them [i.e. the Gauls, the people of the country we now call France] composers of verses whom they call bards; these singing to instruments similar to a lyre, applaud some, while they vituperate others.
>
> They have philosophers and theologians who are held in much honour and are called Druids; they have sooth-sayers [Vates] too of great renown who tell the future by watching the flight of birds and by the observation of the entrails of victims; and every one waits upon their word. ... It is a custom of the Gauls that no one performs a sacrifice without the assistance of a philosopher [i.e. a Druid], for they say that offerings to the gods ought only to be made through the mediation of these men, who are learned in the divine nature and, so to speak, familiar with it, and it is through their agency that the blessings of the gods should properly be sought. It is not only in times of peace, but in war also, that these seers have authority, and the incantations of the bards have effect on friends and foes alike. Often when the combatants are ranged face to face, and swords are drawn and spears bristling, these men come between the armies and stay the battle, just as wild beasts are sometimes held spellbound. Thus even among the most savage barbarians anger yields to wisdom, and Mars is shamed before the Muses.

Diodorus introduces us to the three main areas of Druid practice, those of the bard, ovate and Druid. Each awakens different areas of the self and offers different ways of seeing the world. The path of the bard focuses on finding personal sources of inspiration and awakening creativity. The path of the ovate focuses on healing, awareness and understanding processes of change within ourselves and the world. The path of the Druid seeks to work with the processes of change in order to take a more active role in the continuing process of creation. Modern Druids still act as priests, though nowadays the sacrifices they assist with include such things as time, poetry, seasonal fruits and flowers or mead.

From Pliny and others, we know that ancient Druids conducted rites in forest groves, though this practice may not have been common before Roman attempts to restrict the activities of Druids in the 1st century BCE. At this time Druids had a concept of sacred space called the *nemeton*, an area marked off for ritual use, often surrounded by a bank and ditch earthwork. Sometimes, small temples or shrines were built within the sacred area. Shrines were often wooden structures, though some were of stone, and occasionally of bone; some were square, others circular. Similar shrines were found inside the hilltop towns that were the common form of settlement across Iron Age Europe. Many *nemetonae* contained ritual pits in which offerings were made. Sometimes there were wooden posts or standing stones aligned on sunset or sunrise at significant times of year.

Iron Age Druids used sacred herbs and trees in their rites and practised divination from the behaviour of birds and the movement of stars. Some rites featured music and dancing. Ritual was not the only area in which Druids operated. They were also judges and lawyers, historians, teachers, doctors, singers, musicians. In fact, every aspect of life that required any kind of formal education seems to have been the province of the Druids. They seem to have fulfilled a role among the Iron Age people of Europe similar to the Brahmin caste among Hindus.

The Druidry of this period had its dark side, including animal and probably human sacrifice. This was an age when the people among whom Druids lived and worked were head-hunters, preserving the heads of their enemies as trophies, often using them to decorate shrines. We now seem to be a very long way indeed from the 18th-century romantic image of the white-robed sage. And yet perhaps not so far, since several Classical writers refer to Druids as natural philosophers, astronomers, orators, wise judges, inspired prophets and skilled diplomats. And although the Druids of this period worked closely with death, we know that they held a strong belief in life beyond death, a belief so strong that they celebrated death as a liberation and a rebirth. They also believed in the transmigration of the soul, a belief held by many Druids today.

## Origins

The origins of Druidry are lost in prehistory. The earliest records place Druids among the tribal peoples of Europe identified by modern historians as Celts after one tribal group, the Keltoi. The language and culture we now call Celtic developed in central Europe early in the first millennium BCE, yet Julius Caesar tells us that the Gauls of his time believed that Druidry originated in Britain. It is safe to assume that it developed over thousands of years, its origins going back long before the emergence of the culture we now call Celtic. From the archaeological record it is clear that many ritual practices of the Iron Age Celts were common a thousand years earlier among the Bronze Age builders of the great stone circles of Britain and Ireland and a thousand years earlier still, among the Neolithic folk who built megalithic tomb-shrines like that of New Grange in Ireland. Marking out sacred space with an earthwork bank and ditch, making ritual offerings in pits or shafts and erecting standing stones or wooden posts aligned on sunrise or sunset at certain times of year are all common practices from 3500 BCE to 400 CE.

These then are the bare outlines of Druid history, from the age of the microchip to the age of stone tools. Did you sense the presence of your archetypal Druid at any point on the journey? With which stage in the history of the tradition did you feel the strongest connection? What does that tell you about who you are and what your expectations and desires may be?

So, having made our journey through the past, we bring ourselves back consciously to the present, aware of who we are and of our surroundings. Once we are fully in the here and now, we give thanks to our ancestors of blood and of spirit for all that we have learned, and for all the rich heritage of tradition and teaching that we have inherited from them.

Hail, O ancestors!
Hail and farewell!

# 2

# The Sacred Circle

Whenever we undertake a journey through a landscape that is new to us, a good map is always useful. In Druidry, the sacred circle is the map we use to help us navigate the journey of our lives. At its centre is the axis, the point of perfect balance, stillness, security. Around its rim are all the elements of life and the cycles of time. Because we are all different, we paint our maps in different colours and follow different paths, yet the basic structure of the map remains the same. This chapter describes that structure, showing how to tailor the map to your own needs and how to use it to assess where you have been, locate where you are now and plan future stages of your journey.

As our understanding of Druidry increases, it becomes apparent that what we do operates on many levels; symbol, psyche and soul are woven together within the sacred circle. Having no beginning and no end, the circle symbolises eternity. This symbolism is invoked when we exchange rings during the marriage rite. We invoke the same symbolism when we draw the sacred circle around ourselves, creating the space in which we enter meditation or perform rituals.

As the circle is eternal, so, when we are within it, we place ourselves beyond the normal constraints of time and space. The edge of the circle is a boundary, enclosing that which is within, setting it apart from that which is without. It symbolises protection, strength of purpose, unity and perfection. As well as a boundary, the perimeter of the circle represents a journey through the cycles of time, of sun, moon and stars, of birth, life, death and decay, of the zodiac and of the horizon.

## The Aura: Circle of the Self

At its most fundamental, the sacred circle is simply the area in which our bodies are centred. We each have an aura, or energy field within and around our bodies. Psychics see this aura as an area of coloured light surrounding and interpenetrating the body. The size, strength and colour of the aura change according to physical health, emotional, spiritual or psychic well-being.

In cultures around the world, from ancient Egypt to the present day, the reality of the aura has been accepted among psychics, mystics and healers. In 1939, it entered the realm of science when it was photographed by a Russian electrical engineer, Semyon Davidovitch Kirlian. Professor Kirlian and his wife, Valentina, developed a device which surrounded living objects with high-frequency electrical currents and captured the resulting effect on film. Their technique revealed multicoloured clouds, flares and sparks forming brilliant patterns of light. They demonstrated scientifically the existence of the aura and how it is affected by disease, emotion and other factors, things already known to healers, seers and mystics through the ages. I helped conduct a series of experiments with a type of Kirlian 'camera' in the 1970s.

One clear effect we found was the ability of healers to produce very bright flares from their fingertips when asked to consciously 'turn on' their healing power.

All living things have an aura, even apparently inanimate objects such as rocks. A central tenet of Druidry is animism, the belief that spirit exists within all things. The aura represents a kind of interface, a means of passing information between spirit and physical matter; through the medium of the aura we communicate with everything in our environment. When our own aura comes into contact with another, an interweaving takes place through which messages are passed. For most of us, most of the time, this is an entirely unconscious process, but in Druidry we seek to enhance our ability to communicate. To do this we seek to increase our awareness of the processes involved.

We commonly use only about ten per cent of the capacity of our minds. There are good reasons for this. If our senses were constantly operating at their maximum potential we would be so flooded by incoming sensations that our ability to function would be seriously impaired. If every sound, vision, taste and touch were heightened to a hundred times their usual intensity our minds would be swamped. Simple acts such as driving a car, making a shopping list or even walking would become difficult, if not impossible. However, states of heightened awareness do occur naturally in most people. The psychologist Abraham Maslow called them 'peak experiences' and believed that they represent a register of psychological well-being: the more peak experiences, the healthier the individual. These states are immensely liberating and invigorating, opening the mind to endless vistas of possibility, giving a profound sense of connectedness with the universe, of immense well-being, psychic expansion and spiritual ecstasy. In the practice of Druidry, we seek to access such states of heightened awareness. One stage in this process is to increase awareness of our own personal sacred circle, our auric energy field.

If you relax into awareness of yourself while you are in the midst of a crowd, it is possible to feel how you react to people close to you, even though they may not be physically touching you or talking to you, or even conscious of your presence. You may feel drawn to some, uncomfortable about others. Part of this instinctive reaction is accounted for by non-verbal, usually unconscious signals. Our reactions to people rely heavily on gestures, facial expressions, the way they stand, dress or move. But beyond these responses, we communicate on a deeper level, spirit to spirit, again usually unconsciously. We do this largely through the sensations that filter through to us when our own aura makes contact with another.

## SENSING THE AURA

The following simple exercise can be carried out either alone or in a group and will help to develop awareness.

☆ Sit comfortably with your body balanced, back straight, shoulders relaxed, head centred over your spine and fully supported by it.

☆ Become aware of your physical body, feeling the points at which you touch the floor, then moving your awareness slowly upwards. As you do so, allow your mind to focus on each part of your body, feeling its presence and the sensations flowing from it as fully as you can.

☆ If you sense any discomfort, move until you find the position in which you feel most comfortable. If you find stress or tension in your muscles, allow yourself to become conscious of it then consciously let it go, allowing your body to relax.

☆ When you are satisfied that your whole body is comfortable and supported, hold that sensation for a while, feeling yourself centred within your body. Be aware of your breathing, which should be effortless, slow and even.

☆ Allow your awareness to move beyond your physical body to the area immediately around it, within a few inches of your skin. Working again from the ground up, feel any blockages or areas of discomfort in the auric energy close to your body, just as you did with your physical body. If you come across such problem areas, try to consciously release the tension in them as you did with your physical body.

☆ When you have scanned and processed this part of your aura, move your consciousness outward again. Feel the edge of your auric field, seeking the point at which your own energy interacts with the energy fields of the people or things around you. Become aware of the sensations produced by the interaction, whether they are pleasant or unpleasant, weak or strong, attractive or repellent.

☆ When you feel you have explored these sensations long enough, refocus your consciousness within your body. Be aware of its living, breathing physicality, of your self-awareness centred within it, and of your solid presence in relation to your surroundings.

This exercise helps to develop awareness of different layers of reality, how they interact with each other, how we affect them and how they affect us. It can be performed anywhere and any time, requiring only a little space, time and enough peace, inner and outer, to allow you to focus without distraction. As with most things in life, the more commitment you bring to it, the more you will gain from it.

## Casting the Circle

The sacred circle is a safe space, set apart from the distractions of everyday life, within which we explore ourselves, develop our potential and work through processes of change in our lives. The centre of the circle is the eye of the storm, the point of balance, the fixed axis around which everything revolves. It is this central point that defines the circle. The perimeter of the circle is the interface between the sacred space we create and the rest of creation beyond. Exploring the perimeter from within our sacred circle allows us to work through events in our lives and relationships from a place of safety.

The circle can be formed in many ways, purely through imagination, or by physically marking it with chalk, charcoal, leaves, sticks, sand, stones, earth or anything else that comes to hand and feels appropriate. Often it is simply drawn in the air with the hand or index finger. The circle is usually cast sunwise (clockwise), beginning and ending in the East, the quarter from which the sun rises. Others prefer to cast the circle from the North, the quarter that represents the element of Earth, feeling that this helps to ground their circle and themselves. As important as the physical act of visualising or making a circle is the intention behind it. When drawing a sacred circle, we need to be aware of what it means.

## *Weaving the Web*

Each of us exists at the centre of a web of energy that links us to the rest of creation. Our Scandinavian ancestors called this the Web of Wyrd, conceiving it as the interwoven threads of fate or destiny that link all things in the universe. Often, when we wish for perfect security within our circle, as we draw it we consciously and deliberately cut the threads that link us to the world beyond. This strengthens the circle, preventing anything that might distract from our purpose from entering and, just as importantly, preventing our own psychic energy from leaking out. If this cutting is done, it is essential that the links are restored before the circle is closed (see page 44), otherwise we may find that our relationships with the world are damaged. The process of restoring the threads is referred to as 're-weaving the web'. Both cutting and re-weaving are done with the hands, with clarity of intention. When we make group rituals, we weave together the threads of all those within the circle, strengthening the spirit of the group.

Some see these processes as purely symbolic, while others hold the web to be as objectively real as the clothes we wear or the houses we live in. Others argue that it doesn't matter which view we hold, since symbolic actions affect the psyche and the psyche in turn affects our physical well-being and our relationships. In Druidry, experience is more important than belief.

The perimeter of the circle is the screen on which the dramas of our lives are played out against the backdrop of existence. As we move around the circle, we experience different aspects of ourselves, past, present and potential, and different areas of relationship, tension or release. The journey around the circle is a process of learning about ourselves and our place in the world. Before we begin the journey, we need to populate our circle with images and ideas, to map out the storyboard of our lives.

## The Cardinal Points

We begin this process with the four cardinal points: East, South, West and North; these are our main reference points. They have many potential meanings, and, as in so much of Druidry, the rules are fluid rather than fixed, individual rather than collective. There are, however, basic areas of agreement. For example, most Druids will attribute the four elements to the four points in the same way: Air in the East, Fire in the South, Water in the West and Earth in the North.

**East**  East is the quarter of sunrise and of spring, of birth, childhood, youthful energy and enthusiasm, awakenings and new beginnings. It is associated with the element of Air, with clarity of thought and vision, and lightness of being. In the animal kingdom its associations are naturally with birds, particularly those who sing vigorously at dawn such as the blackbird, those known for clarity of vision such as the hawk or eagle, and those associated with springtime such as the cuckoo.

Mythologically, the East is linked with gods of the air, sunrise and spring. In Irish myth, the young sun god, Lugh of the Long Arm, comes from the East. Lugh's primary weapon is a magical spear that never misses its mark, perhaps a mythical representation of the first shaft of sunlight at dawn. The Spear of Lugh is one of the four treasures of the old gods of Ireland, the *Tuatha de Danaan*, brought by them from their home on the world's rim.

**South**  South is the quarter of summer heat and the midday sun, of power and strength, associated with the element of

Fire, with passion, energy and desire. Animals that express these qualities might include the rutting stag, the wild boar, the fox, the hunting wolf or the wild cat. Otherworld creatures associated with the element of Fire include the dragon, the phoenix and the salamander.

In Irish tradition, the magical weapon of the South is the Sword of *Nuada*, another of the treasures of the old gods. Nuada, like the Welsh *Nudd*, means 'cloud', or 'mist'. Before Nuada of the Silver Hand lost a hand in battle, he was king of the gods. Afterwards, his place was taken by the young sun god, Lugh. At midsummer, Lugh as sun god reaches the height of his power.

**West** West is the region of autumn and the setting sun, of maturity and the wisdom that comes with age and experience. Its element is Water, linked with the emotions, fluidity, mutability and the Otherworld. Its animals are those that dwell in or near water: the heron, swan, turtle, otter, frog, dolphin or whale. The one most commonly invoked in Druidry, though, is the Salmon of Wisdom. Irish myth tells of a well at the centre of the world around which grow nine hazel trees bearing nuts that contain all wisdom. The nuts fall into the well and are eaten by salmon. Anyone lucky enough to catch and eat one of these salmon gains knowledge of things past, present and future.

In Irish tradition, the magical treasure of the West is the Cauldron of the Dagda, the father of the gods. This cauldron is inexhaustible, and everyone who comes to it finds exactly what they want; those who bathe in it have their wounds healed, and it can restore the dead to life. In Welsh tradition, the magical vessel is the Cauldron of Inspiration (Awen), in which the goddess Ceridwen brews a broth that gives the gifts of poetry, prophecy and shape-shifting.

**North**   North is the place of dark night and winter cold, of old age, death and decay, dormancy and hibernation, the quarter from which sun and moon never shine. Its element is Earth, its qualities physicality, solidity, stability and endurance. Its animals include the bear, bull, badger, sow, raven, crow, owl and bat.

In Irish tradition, the magical treasure of the North is the Lia Fail, the Stone of Destiny, the ancient coronation stone of the high kings of Ireland that used to scream in recognition of the true king. Goddesses associated with the North include the Irish hag trinity of Badb, Macha and the Morrigan, who transform themselves into ravens to choose those who die in battle and to feast on their corpses. In Welsh tradition, a god of the North is Gwynn ap Nudd, 'White son of Cloud', the horseman who leads the Wild Hunt of the souls of the dead through the night on their journey to the Otherworld.

## Making Your Own Map

Some of the attributions suggested above may be inappropriate for you. If, for example, you live on the east coast of Scotland, looking out across the wild North Sea, it might not make much sense for you to attribute the element of Water to the West. Similarly, if you live in Western Australia, it would defy logic to place cold, dark winter in the North when that is the direction from which the sun shines at noon. Working with the sacred circle, develop your own associations. Your map will become much more effective as you construct it in ways that have meaning for you.

From the centre of your sacred circle, face each of the four cardinal points in turn, thinking about what they mean to you personally. Perhaps you have suffered painful burns. If so, you might associate the South with pain. Or your feeling about the element of Fire might have more to do with the warmth of hearth and home. Feelings may intermingle. Fear of drowning may give negative associations with Water, but you might also love the sound of waterfalls. You might relate the element of Earth to strength and stability, or to darkness, claustrophobia or your dislike of winter cold. Establishing a personal map of such correspondences makes your sacred circle unique.

## Working with the Circle

Having cast your circle and become familiar with the four directions you can begin to work with them. Move to each of the cardinal points in turn and see how your feelings change as you align yourself with the elemental and other qualities of each quarter. You might feel uncomfortable in one quarter, secure in another, enlivened in another. Analysing these positive and negative responses can offer insight into your present state of being. Do you feel a lack of energy? If so, you might need to attune yourself with the element of Fire in the South. Do you feel insecure? Perhaps you need the stability of the element of Earth in the North. Are you stressed? Perhaps you need to bathe in the cool waters of the West. Lacking clarity? The answer may lie with the clear light of dawn in the East.

There are many ways to connect with the elemental powers of the quarters. Facing the appropriate direction and consciously opening yourself to its gifts is simple and effective. Or you might choose an animal associated with the quarter and awaken its attributes in yourself, perhaps through imitating its actions and cries. Don't feel embarrassed, no one is watching! Exploration is the key. Being attuned to your own responses as you move around the circle will lead you to find your own ways of working.

We call to the powers of the quarters as we make our sacred circle. When we do this, we call to our ritual space those qualities and energies we feel we need or that are appropriate to the work we are doing. An example of a call to the North might be:

> Spirits of the North, spirits of Earth, I call to you. Brown Bull of the North, I ask for your strength and determination. Bear Mother, I ask for your nurturing warmth, your protectiveness. Raven of Winter and dark night, I ask for your hidden wisdom. May these gifts of the powers of the North be present in this circle, that those gathered here may know them. Spirits of the North, spirits of Earth, I bid you hail and welcome!

For examples of calls to each of the quarters, see Chapter 7. Bear in mind that the ritual texts given in this book are merely suggestions. Your rites will be more potent if the words you use are your own, clearly expressing your own understanding and intention.

## The Wheel of the Year

Through the links we make with the four cardinal points, we anchor our circle within the world, aware of its place in the web of relationships, of which each of us is the centre. Quartering the circle gives us the symbol known as the Celtic cross. Building on this four-fold foundation, we further sub-divide the circle by adding the cross-quarters to our map. This gives us the image of an eight-spoked wheel. Taking the perimeter of the circle to represent the cycle of the sun through the year, the points at which the spokes meet the rim mark the eight major festivals celebrated in modern Druidry.

In celebrating these festivals within the sacred circle, we align ourselves with the cycles of the natural world reflected in the changing seasons.

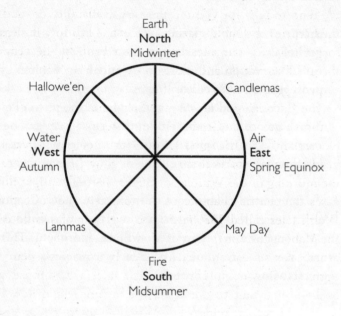

The Wheel of the Year

## Midwinter

Our journey around the wheel's rim begins at the North, the dark of the moon, midnight, Midwinter. The Winter Solstice, falling on or about 21 December, is the shortest day of the year. In Wales it is called *Alban Arthan*, the Light of the Great Bear, after the most prominent constellation in the northern sky. Our ancestors celebrated Midwinter a few days after the actual Solstice, on 25 December. At dawn on that day, the point at which the sun rises on the horizon begins to move northward, offering the first sign of the slow return from winter to spring and summer. Our ancestors characterised this as the rebirth of the sun. In industrialised nations, we tend to take for granted the easy availability of food and the luxuries of double-glazing and central heating. It's easy to forget that, for our ancestors, winter brought the very real threat of starvation and death; no wonder the rebirth of the sun was greeted with celebration.

The Egyptian god Horus, the Babylonian Baal, the Persian Mithras and the Greek Adonis were all born on 25 December. The Irish god Lugh of the Long Arm was born inside the prehistoric tomb-shrine of New Grange where, on the morning of the Winter Solstice, a shaft of sunlight illuminates the central chamber of the tomb. In the collection of Welsh tales called *The Mabinogion*, we hear of a child called the Mabon (the Son), born of Modron (the Mother). This and other tales reflect an ancient belief in a magical solar child born at Midwinter. Through such tales we glimpse what Midwinter meant to our ancestors: a time when new birth emerged from the midst of death and decay, of consciousness emerging from the dark comfort of the womb, open to a flood of new experiences, yet helpless and reliant on others for protection and nourishment. In particular, as newborn children, we rely on our mothers. The nurturing arms of the mother, the comfort and security of the womb, are associated with the North. Our ancestors viewed death as a return to the womb of Mother Earth. In the North, then, we find both the end and the beginning of life.

## Candlemas

Moving sunwise around the circle, we come to the North-East, where the elements of Earth and Air combine. This marks the first of the cross-quarter days, Candlemas, falling on 1/2 February. This is celebrated as *Imbolc* in Ireland and as *Gwyl Forwyn*, the Feast of the Virgin, in Wales. It marks the time when ewes begin to lactate and the first wild flowers appear, heralding the coming spring. It is traditionally a celebration of lights, with candles being lit to illuminate churches and homes. As at the other quarter days, offerings of food and drink, particularly milk, are put out for the Faery Folk or poured over standing stones. In Scottish folklore, Candlemas is the time when a white snake, the Serpent of Bride, emerges from underground where it has spent the winter months. The serpent is a potent image of life returning to the land. Bride, or Brigid, is an ancient goddess of fertility, poetry and smithcraft whose worship was transferred to a Christian saint with the same name.

The child born at Midwinter has now grown, but is still reliant on its mother and father for nourishment and protection. The child now begins to recognise boundaries and differences between itself and the world. This is the first step towards independence of thought and being.

## Spring Equinox

East marks the Spring Equinox, the Welsh *Alban Eilir*, the Light of Regeneration, which falls on or about 21 March. The sun is then just entering the zodiacal sign of Aries, the Ram. On the morning of the Equinox, the sun rises directly in the East. Day and night are of equal length; it is a time of balance between the long nights of winter and the long days of summer. Balance is a temporary state and, at this time, it is about to tip in favour of summer. In human terms it is the time when the child begins to develop as an individual, independent of its parents, still wide-eyed with wonderment but no longer content just to observe. Now the child is eager to experience all that the world has to offer.

## May Day

Moving sunwise again, we come to the second cross-quarter day at the South-East: 1 May, May Day. In Ireland, this is still celebrated as *Beltaine*, a folk festival at which twin fires were lit on hilltops and cattle were driven between the fires to protect them from disease. In Wales the festival is called *Calan Mai*, May Calends. In Britain and elsewhere May Day is celebrated by choosing a young girl to be Queen of the May, by decking churches with seasonal flowers and dancing around Maypoles. It is seen as the first day of summer and the end of winter. In some folk rituals a battle is acted out between the forces of winter, sometimes represented by a man dressed as a woman, and those of summer, often led by the May Queen or her consort. May Eve is a traditional time for young men and women to go to the greenwood to make love. At dawn, women bathe their faces in May morning dew to renew, enhance or preserve their youth and beauty. Young people gather May flowers, particularly hawthorn blossom, for use in the revels of the day.

The South-East is the midpoint between Air and Fire, a volatile mix appropriate to this celebration of youthful vigour. It is here that we reach puberty, the sexual awakening that marks the passage from childhood to adulthood. For many, it is a time of wild excitement, but also of great tension as we struggle to come to terms with a host of new sensations. It is a time of change and upheaval, shot through with the passionate energy of youth.

## Midsummer

As the wheel turns we come to the South, the place of Midsummer. The Summer Solstice falls on or about 21 June and is called *Alban Hefin,* the Light of Summer, in Wales. As at Midwinter, the sun's rising position remains still. Midsummer's Day falls a few days later, on 24 June, when the sunrise position begins to move southward again. As at *Beltaine*, Midsummer was traditionally celebrated with hilltop fires. Wheels were set on fire and rolled downhill. How well they burned, how far and fast they rolled, and how high they bounced, indicated the fortunes of the community through the coming year.

At the South of the circle, the child has become an adult, retaining the energy of youth but with the strength of body and will to transform desire into action. Strong desire and the energy to achieve can be very attractive, but can also lead to conflict. In the fiery South, conflict is welcomed for the opportunity it gives to display strength, courage, dominance and determination. Yet if conflict is uncontained or misdirected, great harm can ensue. At the pivotal point of the Solstice, the power is too wild, hence our ancestors celebrated Midsummer a few days later when energies had cooled a little.

## Lammas

Moving on to the South-West we come to the point at which Fire and Water meet. The festival of this cross-quarter is Lammas, celebrated on 1 August. In Ireland it is called *Lughnasad*, the Festival of Lugh, in Wales it is *Gwyl Awst*, the August Feast. It is a celebration of the first fruits of the harvest, a time to give thanks for the magical conjunction of earth, air, rain and sun that produces the food we eat. Our ancestors feasted at this time, both in thanksgiving and in preparation for the hard work of the harvest that still lay ahead. Lammas was a traditional time for pilgrimages to sacred sites. Our ancestors also organised games and races at Lammas, giving young hot-heads a chance to let off steam while they entertained and were cheered on by the rest of the community. Finally, Lammas is a traditional time for celebrating marriage. This reflects the idea of youthful passions giving way to maturity, to thoughts of settling down and raising a family.

At this point in the cycle the flaming passion of the hero begins to cool as the desire for action is tempered by the beginnings of wisdom. Our focus shifts away from pure self-interest and we begin to develop an understanding of the needs of others, a sense of compassion and of community.

## Autumn Equinox

In the West we reach the fall of the year, the Autumn Equinox, on or about 21 September. In Wales it is called *Alban Elfed*, the Light of Autumn. As at the Spring Equinox, day and night are of equal length and we are at a point of balance. Now, though, the balance is about to tip from summer, the season of growth, into winter, a time of decay and dormancy. The harvest has been gathered in and stored against the coming cold, and trees and hedgerows are heavy with fruit. The work of harvest done, there is time to rest, reflect, celebrate, give thanks, and to prepare for the cold months ahead.

In the cycle of our lives, we have achieved the wisdom of age. The struggle is past and we can rest and take stock, deciding which aspects of ourselves have real and lasting value, which we no longer need. In the terminology of the harvest, we separate the wheat from the chaff.

## Hallowe'en

The wheel rolls on, bringing us to the North-West and the festival of Hallowe'en, known in Ireland as *Samhain*, in Wales as *Nos Galan Gaeaf*, the Night of Winter Calends. It falls on 31 October and represents the conjunction of Water and Earth. At this time of year, our ancestors brought their herds down from the summer pastures, slaughtering excess livestock that they were unable to feed through the winter. As at May Day, its opposite on the wheel of the year, Hallowe'en fires were lit on hilltops and cattle driven between them for protection and blessing. In parts of Wales, when the fires died down, every-one would run home helter-skelter while the cry went up: 'The Tailless Black Sow take the hindmost!'

Of all nights of the year, Hallowe'en is when ghoulies, gheesties and long leggity beasties are out in force. Witches fly the skies on broomsticks, making their way to the greatest Sabbat of the year, while Gwyn ap Nudd, or his Saxon coun-terpart, Woden, rides the night at the head of the Wild Hunt, leading the souls of the dead towards their long rest.

Our ancestors placed lighted candles in their windows to welcome home the spirits of the dead; they put out offerings of food and set places at their tables for relatives who had died. It was a trickster night when pranks were played on neighbours, with animal disguises and cross-dressing adding to the playful chaos. Why? Because this, again along with May Day, is one of the great thresholds of the year. Hallowe'en marks the divide between summer and winter. On this night, the gateway between the worlds of flesh and of spirit is wide open. Through the games, tricks and disguises that marked the festival, our ancestors faced the darkness with humour, imagination and courage.

In the cycle of our lives, the North-West represents old age and death. We sense the coming darkness, aware at last of our own mortality, and make our final decisions about what we are content to leave behind, and what we will carry with us into the darkness. Aware of our frailty and the long road that lies ahead, we know we must choose only those things we value most.

The final part of our journey takes us back to where we began: the womb-like peace of the North from which we are reborn to begin the cycle again. So the whole of life is encompassed within the sacred circle.

In marking out the circle around us and cutting the threads that link us to the world beyond its edge, we make the circle a place of perfect safety. By walking its rim with clear intention, we find those areas of our life where we may have experienced pain, sorrow, joy, clarity, fear, jealousy, inspiration, anger, peace, disillusion, love, embarrassment, hatred or kindness. Through reliving these experiences within the safety of the circle, we learn about ourselves, our weaknesses and strengths, hopes and fears, sources of inspiration and those things that hold us back.

There are life experiences and negative self-images that can prevent us from fulfilling our potential; the sacred circle offers us the opportunity to work through these blockages. Often, the simple act of facing such problem areas in our psyche within the circle offers its own solutions. Other blockages might require more work in order to overcome them. As with our experience of the four elements, walking the eightfold wheel with awareness, attuned to our own feelings and responses, can often present its own answers to difficulties.

This exercise is about locating areas of tension, then finding the point of release that will free you to move on. Used well, with focus and understanding, it is one of the most powerful tools in Druidry.

## Walking the Circle

☆ Once a problem area in life has been recognised, cast your circle as described, sunwise from East to East.

☆ When it is cast, go to each of the quarters in turn, beginning at the East and moving clockwise to the South, West and North, returning again to the East. At each quarter, invite into the circle those positive qualities that you feel you need.

☆ Now move to the middle of the circle and centre yourself, using the 'Sensing the Aura' exercise on page 25.

☆ From the centre, try to find where your problem lies on the rim of the circle. A problem with male dominance might lie in the South; an emotional problem might surface in the West; a sexual problem in the South-East; a problem with social interactions in the South-West.

☆ Once you have found where on the circle your problem lies, move to that place and let yourself go as deep as you can into the problem, feeling how it affects you personally. If this is uncomfortable, remember that you are within the safety of sacred space, and that you have full control over what you invite into your circle and what you allow to leave it. Try not to dismiss the discomfort or ignore it, but really feel it.

☆ Ask your guides, whether you view them as aspects of your psyche or self-existent beings, to help you understand the root causes of the problem. When you feel that you have understood all that you can about the nature of the problem and its causes within yourself, think about how it affects others around you.

☆ When you have immersed yourself in all aspects of the problem, you are ready to look for solutions. Often these can be found by moving around the circle to the next stage of the cycle. So, if your problem is with male dominance in the South, the solution may lie in the maturity and sense of community that emerges in the South-West. If the answer fails to emerge through moving around the circle, it will often be found by looking across the circle to the opposite point on the perimeter. So, if the problem is that you are lost in emotional turmoil, the West is the place of emotion. Its opposite is the East, the quarter of Air, the mind, clarity and new beginnings.

☆ When you think you have located the solution to your problem, walk the circle to that point. When your reach it, allow yourself to dive into your feelings again, and imagine how you might put the solution into action and what results it might have for yourself and those around you. You may be certain that your chosen course of action is right. You may not. If you have doubts after exploring all the possibilities, go back and begin the process again.

☆ Return to the point at which you located the problem and immerse yourself in it again. Then look for other possible solutions. Having found where they lie on the circle, move again and test out your new ideas. Repeat the process as many times as you need until you are sure that you know what you need to do to move your life forward.

## CLOSING THE SACRED CIRCLE

Having created a sacred circle, it must always be closed when the work within it is done. If a circle is not consciously closed, the psyche can remain tied to the processes undergone in the circle, failing to return fully into its relationship with the world beyond the circle.

☆ Before closing the circle, give thanks to the ancestors, to your gods and guides, for all that you have learned and experienced. Go to each quarter again, beginning in the North and moving counter-clockwise through West and South, ending in the East. Give thanks for the elemental qualities you called for at the beginning of the rite. Suggested forms of words for each of the quarters are given in Chapter 7. Again, it is better if you speak your own words, clearly reflecting your own feelings. The following example is given for guidance:

> Spirits of the North, spirits of Earth, Brown Bull,
> Bear Mother, Raven of Winter, I thank you for the
> gifts of strength, security and wisdom you have
> brought to this circle. May they remain with us as
> we now bid you hail and farewell!

☆ Then close the circle by erasing it, either physically or in your imagination, depending on how it was made. Begin at the North and move counter-clockwise through West, South and East, ending at the North. If you have 'cut the threads' as described, you should re-weave them.

☆ As you close the circle, be aware of coming back fully and consciously into the everyday world.

☆ Finally, give thanks to the spirits of place, thanking them for accepting your presence.

The rite is now ended.

# Part II

# Inspiration and Creativity: The Path of the Bard

# 3

# The Flowing Spirit

At the heart of Druid practice is the quest for inspiration. Inspiration is the food and drink of the soul. It gives strength to the body, courage to the heart, knowledge, wisdom and insight to the mind, and ecstasy to the spirit. In the British Druid tradition, the spirit of inspiration is called Awen. Awen is a feminine noun, variously translated as 'muse', 'genius', 'inspiration', 'poetic furore', and 'poetic frenzy'. It is made up of two words: 'aw', meaning 'flowing', and 'en', meaning 'spirit'. So, literally, Awen is the 'flowing spirit'.

The concept of Awen is fascinating. I first encountered it in the poetry of medieval Welsh bards; the *Story of Taliesin* helped me to realise just how central Awen is to the understanding and practice of Druidry. In the story, a child called Gwion Bach, 'Little Innocent', inadvertently drinks three drops from a cauldron of inspiration (i.e. Awen) brewed by the goddess Ceridwen. Through these magic drops he gains three gifts: poetry, prophecy and shape-shifting. These are gifts that define the three areas of Druidic practice: poetry for the bard, prophecy for the ovate and shape-shifting for the Druid. Medieval British bards describe the goddess

Ceridwen, whose name means 'crooked woman' or 'bent white one', as the patroness of their order.

In Ireland, the nearest equivalent to Awen is Dana, variously translated as 'a gift', 'a treasure', 'a spiritual offering or gift', 'art', 'science', 'calling' or 'the art of poetry'. This is seen as a gift of the goddess Brighid, described in a 9th-century manuscript as: 'a poet and a goddess worshipped by poets on account of the generous protection afforded them by her'.

Like Shakti in Hindu tradition, Awen is the active power of creation; it is an energy that takes many forms, manifesting particularly through a goddess who is its origin and its agent.

From early medieval times Irish bards have referred to inspiration as a fire in the head. Others, like the Welsh Taliesin, see it in liquid form, and yet others as breath or bread, the fundamentals of life. Always it is seen as a tangible substance that we can reach out and grasp if we try. In our culture we tend to see inspiration as a force beyond our understanding or control that falls at random on lucky individuals at certain times, enabling them to create music, art, literature or some new scientific process. To the Druid bard, inspiration – Awen – is a power we can learn to access at will.

> *The Awen I sing,*
> *from the deep I bring it,*
> *A river while it flows,*
> *I know its extent;*
> *I know when it disappears,*
> *I know when it fills;*
> *I know when it overflows;*
> *I know when it spills.*

## Sensing the Awen

To begin to understand the flow of Awen, we first need to learn to sense its presence. One way to do this is to become fully aware of the physical and psychic sensations that the products of other people's inspiration produce in us. The poet Robert Graves said that true poetry made the hairs on the back of his neck stand up. A Van Gogh painting in a gallery in Amsterdam produced a feeling that caused my body to become weightless and insubstantial, and there are ancient sacred sites that produce a tingling in my palms like static electricity, while others generate a sensation of heat and tautness in my solar plexus. Some people become short of breath, others find that their heart rate slows or speeds up. Our responses to the presence of the spirit are as different as we are from each other and may vary in ourselves from moment to moment. Sometimes we respond with simple awe.

Explore your own responses. Immerse yourself in whatever art form you find most inspirational: a painting, a chamber concert, a David Bowie gig, a forest, hilltop or sacred site, a favourite piece of music, poem, passage from a novel, or a film. While engaged in the experience, look for the physical and psychic reactions that are your personal response to the spirit of inspiration. Be aware of how you feel before and after the experience. If you are left feeling elated, open, free, connected, pleasantly intoxicated or high, rising on a good day towards ecstasy and beyond, then the chances are you have had a genuine encounter with Awen. If, on the other hand, you feel deflated, dispirited, bored or confused, maybe you should consider changing your taste!

In Druidry there are many ways in which we seek to bring Awen, inspiration, into our lives. The arts are a rich source, the natural world is another. Again, our responses are individual. The sight, sound and scent of the sea are intoxicating to some, while others find their deepest inspiration in the quiet depths of the forest or on a high hilltop in the midst of a thunderstorm. Some bloom under the heat of the summer sun, others respond more powerfully to the changing faces of the cool moon. Some find enchantment in the colourful flash of the kingfisher, others in the patient solitude of the heron, the ghostly, silent flight of the hunting barn owl, or the soaring freedom of the mountain eagle. Some revel in the self-satisfied purr of a contented cat, others find their soul's reflection in the lone wanderings or pack protectiveness of the wolf, the strength of buffalo or bear, the regal authority of the stag, or the quick movements of the roebuck. Trees too can inspire: the dark and ancient wisdom of the yew, the epic grandeur of tall pines, the strength and stability of the oak, the fluid flexibility of willow, and the prickly beauty of may or blackthorn. Leaves, flowers, the colour and texture of dark loam or golden sand, the quicksilver of moonlight on water, the tumbling roar of a waterfall, the gentle burble of a woodland stream, the flicker of firelight, the ever-changing shapes of clouds, summer rain or winter snows; all can be potent sources of inspiration, creating the same kinds of physical, psychological and spiritual responses that we find in art.

We recognise and honour these sources of inspiration in ritual. For example, we may say something similar to the following when the circle is cast:

> *The circle is unbroken,*
> *the ancestors awoken.*
> *May the songs of the Earth*
> *and of her people ring true.*
> *Hail to the spirits of this place:*
> *of root and branch, tooth and claw,*

*fur and feather, of earth and sea and sky.*
*Hail and welcome!*

## Chanting the Awen

In shared rites and personal practice we often invoke Awen simply by chanting the word itself. In group ritual we do this to draw inspiration into the participants and the circle. This enables each individual to give and receive more fully, strongly and clearly within the context of the rite. Making the chant as a group has the effect of pooling the inspiration of the individual members, creating a spiritual cauldron of inspiration that all may drink from. In personal practice the Awen may be chanted when we have particular need of inspiration, either for some creative project or to find the answer to a problem. Usually, the chant will be made within the environment of the sacred circle.

Traditionally, the Awen is chanted either three times or in multiples of three. Sometimes a chant will simply run on until it ends naturally. In groups, it is not necessary for everyone to chant in unison, indeed the quality of the sound is richer and more multitextured if the different voices start at different times. The intonation is often pitched low, producing a distinct vibration deep in the belly. Raising the pitch takes the vibration up into the chest or the head. Experimentation will establish what works best for you under what circumstances. Each syllable is extended for as long as your breath will allow.

### SEEKING AWEN

The purpose of the following exercise is to help you to identify personal sources of inspiration and, perhaps, to find some new things to add to your altar.

☆ Cast your circle as described in the previous chapter. You may want to light a candle on your altar or burn some incense. Experiment to find what you need to do to create an atmosphere conducive to spiritual practice.

☆ Settle down before the altar. Sit comfortably, spine straight and supporting your head well. Now, focus clearly on the intention of the rite: to increase your knowledge of yourself and your sources of inspiration.

☆ Take a couple of deep, slow breaths and let them out again slowly. With the third intake of breath, begin the Awen chant, repeating the word three times. The sound of the chant is: 'Aaaaaaaaa-oooooooooo-eeeeeeeee-nnnnnnnnn' ('a' as in father, 'oo' as in moon, 'e' as in when).

☆ As you chant, be aware of the physical, psychic and spiritual effects the process has on you. When you have completed the chant, sit still for a few moments, allowing the resonance of the sound to permeate yourself and the space around you.

☆ When you are ready, get up and open a gateway in your circle. You may do this by putting the palms of your hands together, sliding them into the rim of your circle and then moving them apart, as if you are parting a pair of curtains. Otherwise, you may draw a doorway in the air. Step through and close the gateway you have made. This may seem a curious process, but it has the effect of maintaining the 'seal' on your sacred space. It is also a physical reminder that sacred space *is* sacred and therefore worthy of respect.

☆ Now, go out into the world and look for some small, portable object that inspires you. Don't look too consciously or too hard. Act from the belly, not the head. Be open, free from preconceptions. Go wherever instinct takes you and find whatever you are led to by it.

☆ When you have found something, bring it back with you: open your circle, as described, before entering it, close it behind you and resume your place before the altar.

☆ Hold the object in your hands and focus on it, allowing your mind to wander down whatever avenues of thought are awakened by it. If you find yourself drifting off into idle thoughts, use the physical presence of the object to bring you back to focus. Examine every aspect of it: its texture, shape, colour, smell and taste. What thoughts, sensations, feelings and impressions do these things evoke in you? After following each chain of association as far as it will go, return again to the object. In this way you will expand your knowledge of the object itself, of yourself and your responses to it, of the sources of your inspiration and, if you allow the meditation to carry you far enough, of the structure and meaning of the universe.

Every material object is composed of particles with space in between through which energies flow. These cause the particles to move in a patterned dance that determines whether the basic building blocks of existence manifest as wood, water, silk or stone. This web of energies, mirroring the Web of Wyrd, links all things together. Through it, the infinitely small relates to the infinitely large, the energies moving out from each pebble, flower or grain of sand connect to every other, and then reach out from the Earth to touch the Moon and Sun, and beyond them to the stars and distant galaxies, on to the very edge of the universe where time and space cease to exist, just as they do here, within the sacred circle.

☆ When the object of your meditation has taken you as far as it can, it is time to give thanks for what you have learned and close the circle. You should know by this time whether your object is something to make space for on your altar. If it is, take an offering back to the place where you found it and offer it, with thanks, to the spirit of the place. Offerings should be such that they will leave no trace after a few hours or days: food that birds or animals may eat, drink that will soak into the earth, flowers that will rot down, releasing nutrients into the soil.

☆ If you decide not to keep the object, take it back to the place where you found it and replace it carefully. You may leave an offering for the spirit of the place, or you may give the object itself, and the time and effort it has taken to return it as your offering.

## The Cell of Song

A traditional method of awakening the flow of Awen was practised in the bardic colleges of Ireland, Scotland and Wales and was known as 'the Cell of Song'. Bards were given a subject on which to compose a poem. Then they were shut up alone in dark, windowless cells for a day and a night. All that time the bards would lay on their beds, often with their heads swathed in cloth to enhance sensory deprivation. In the darkness, removed from all distraction, the mind roams free, entering a state between dream and waking where associations that normal consciousness would miss or dismiss may be pursued along paths of thought to remote, often wildly illogical conclusions. The normal sensory defences crumble as the hours go by, enabling the Awen to flow free.

After 24 hours, the bards were brought candles and wrote down the poems they had created. The class then reassembled and the poems were offered for assessment. The quality of the verses gave a clear indication of the extent to which each bard had connected with the Awen.

This is one reason why, in Druidry, we use our inspiration to create: so that our inspiration can be judged by others through the quality of our creations. This can be a scary process, but it encourages us to constantly refine and improve what we do. Also, the products of our creativity serve as offerings in exchange for the inspiration we receive. So is the flow of Awen maintained.

## Creative Dreaming

Dreams can be a fruitful source of inspiration that can be translated into poetry, painting, story or song. Keep a diary at your bedside and record your dreams on waking each morning. Doing this regularly will enable you to recall more and more of your dreams. As in the Cell of Song, sleep frees the mind from its normal constraints, allowing messages that would otherwise be blocked to come through. Many dreams are simply the mind's way of sifting and processing data received during waking hours. Others may carry recollections of past lives, intimations of the future or messages from your ancestors, gods and guides. Either way, the dream world often produces rich and strange imagery that can be woven into expressions of creativity. Dreams inspire not only poets and artists; many scientists find insights and visions in dreams that help them solve problems in their work.

So, dream on!

# 4

# Ancestral Voices

Our ancestors communicate with us through songs and poetry, legend and lore passed down by generations of bards. As we walk the path of Druidry, we come across many such doorways through which we can enter the realm of the ancestors, the realm of spirit. That magical Otherworld exists, eternal and ever-changing, alongside our own, and in it all things are possible. The stories, songs and poetry of our ancestors provide such doorways. Through the magic of words we link ourselves, heart, mind and soul, with the Awen, the flowing spirit, of those who created them.

Stories, songs and poems are the stock-in-trade of the bard. Bards are keepers of tradition, remodelling history into stories that teach and inspire, capable of both holding and moving an audience. In this way, history is transformed into the myths and legends that inform our sense of personal and cultural identity, providing the backdrop to our existence, our beliefs, our sense of self, our connection with the past and the sacred land. Stories and songs are our teachers. Through them we learn about correct behaviour, the beliefs of our ancestors, the nature of the gods, the Otherworld and its inhabitants.

In traditional bardic performances, story, song and poetry were often combined. Two bards would work together, one taking the vocals while the other accompanied on that archetypal bardic instrument, the harp.

For example, *The Voyage of Bran* is an 8th-century tale of the type called *imramma* or voyages, the telling of which as a sacred act guides the listener on a journey to the Otherworld – experience and knowledge of which are central to the Druidic tradition. I believe they were sung at the bedside of those who were dying, providing guidance for their souls' journey to the Islands of the Earthly Paradise. Bran was an Irish king who was visited in his hall by a strangely dressed and beautiful woman who sang to him the following description of her Otherworld home.

> *I bring a branch of Emain's apple tree,*
> *alike in form to those you know.*
> *Twigs of white silver upon it grow*
> *and buds of crystal blossom fair to see.*
>
> *There is an island far beyond this land,*
> *around which glisten white sea-horses.*
> *Against its shores they flow their white courses,*
> *upon four pillars strong that island stands.*
>
> *An ancient tree there is in flower,*
> *whereon bright birds each hour call.*
> *In sweetest harmony they all*
> *combine to sing the passing of each hour.*
>
> *No sorrow known, nor grieving there,*
> *no sickness, death or suffering.*

*Such is the life of fair Emain,*
*a life that in this world is all too rare.*

*A host then comes across the shining sea*
*and row their craft most skilfully to land,*
*to where the shining stones in circles stand,*
*from which arise a music sweet and free.*

*Through ages long unto the gathered throng*
*they sing a song that sorrow never stained;*
*a hundred voices, all in chorus reigned,*
*in praise of life and life's eternal song.*

*Emain of many shapes beside the sea,*
*whether it be far or it be near,*
*women in bright colours wander here,*
*surrounded by the clear and shining sea.*

*And if you hear the sweet voice of the stones*
*and the songbirds of the Peaceful Land,*
*those women will walk close at hand;*
*no one who comes need walk alone.*

The verses, more than 1,000 years old, give a vivid impression of how our ancestors pictured the Otherworld, the Faery realm beyond the western ocean to which the soul travels after death.

Other poems recall non-human transformations, suggesting that Awen awakened the bard to heightened states of awareness where consciousness merged with the universe and everything in it. This is the same state which the exercise on page 52 may help you achieve. So, in 'The Battle of the Trees', the bard Taliesin sings:

*I have been in many shapes*
*Before I took this congenial form;*
*I have been a sword, narrow in shape;*
*I believe, since it is apparent,*
*I have been a tear-drop in the sky,*
*I have been a glittering star,*
*I have been a word in a letter,*
*I have been a book in my origin,*
*I have been a gleaming ray of light,*
*A year and a half,*
*I have been a stable bridge*
*Over confluences of compassion,*
*I have been a pathway, I have been an eagle,*
*I have been a coracle on the brink,*
*I have been the direction of a staff,*
*I have been a stack in an open enclosure,*
*I have been a sword in a yielding cleft,*
*I have been a shield in open conflict,*
*I have been a string on a harp,*
*Shape-shifting nine years,*
*In water, in foam,*
*I have been consumed in fire,*
*I have been passion in a covert.*

This expression of universality reminds us that, among our forebears, bards were regarded with the same kind of awe and reverence reserved in other cultures for priests, medicine men or wise women. In our own day there is still a kind of mystical aura attached to the creative arts, a sense that those who practise them are connected to some inner source that sets them apart from the rest of humanity. We recognise this source as Awen.

## Many Blessings

Among our ancestors, a visit from a bard was held to convey blessings on a house, its inhabitants, their crops and livestock. Traditional tales themselves were believed to bestow blessings on the teller and the hearer. Saint Patrick, patron saint of Ireland, is said to have ordered that no one should sleep or talk while one tale was being told, and promised that it would bring success with children, love, marriage, legal matters or hunting, protection to seafarers, peace in banqueting halls and freedom for those held captive. Such blessings are reminiscent of those promised to one who recites or listens to Hindu sacred tales such as the *Ramayana*. The recitation of these tales is more than mere storytelling, it is a magical rite and a religious mystery, for the blessings offered are the same as those otherwise conferred by prayer or sacrifice to the gods.

## Tales of the Gods

Traditional storytellers speak of being aware of previous generations of storytellers standing behind them while recounting one of the old tales. By allowing ourselves to be open to these spirits of our predecessors, we can learn more about the stories, perhaps recovering parts that have been lost.

Myths reveal the nature of the gods, their births, their powers, how they relate to humankind, and how we may relate to them. They can suggest where and when rituals should be performed, since they often identify specific places and times associated with a particular deity. For example, the Irish goddess Brighid is associated with a sanctuary in County Kildare where a perpetual flame burned in her honour, and with Tober Breda, a holy well in County Cork. The Christian saint Brigit, who took over the role of her pagan predecessor, had her feast day on 1 February, the festival of *Imbolc*. The British goddess, Ceridwen, is associated with Bala Lake in North Wales, and gave birth to her son, the magical bard Taliesin, on 29 April, the eve of the festival of *Calan Mai*.

## Cycles of the Sun

Many myths seem to trace the life cycle of a sun god from birth at Midwinter, through to the height of his strength at Midsummer and to his death at *Samhain*. The events of this cycle are usually driven by the relationship of the god to one or more goddesses. One example is the Welsh legend of Lleu Llaw Gyffes, which forms part of the tale of Math, son of Mathonwy, featured in the collection of medieval Welsh legends known as *The Mabinogion*. This tells how Arianrhod, 'Silver Wheel', gives birth to Lleu, 'Light', and his twin brother, Dylan ap Ton, 'Ocean son of Wave', as she steps over a staff held by Math, a shadowy enchanter. Since Lleu is a sun god, his birth is most likely to have taken place at Midwinter, when the sun has passed its low point at the Winter Solstice and thus been reborn.

Lleu is taken by Gwydion ap Don, 'Lord of the Wildwood', the archetypal Druid of Welsh tradition. His mother, Arianrhod, lays a curse on him that he shall never have a name unless she herself gives one to him. Gwydion and Lleu return to Arianrhod's castle in a boat, from which Lleu shoots an arrow through the leg of a wren. Arianrhod comments: 'The light-haired one has a steady hand.' This gives the child his name: Lleu Llaw Gyffes, 'Light of the Steady Hand', and in turn brings us to *Gwyl Forwyn* (Irish

*Imbolc*, Candlemas, 1/2 February), a festival associated with light and with the suckling of young lambs.

Arianrhod then says that he will never bear arms unless she herself arms him. Gwydion therefore magically creates the sound of an army surrounding the castle, causing Arianrhod to arm her guests, including Lleu. The arming of the young god seems appropriate to the Spring Equinox (Welsh *Alban Eilir*, the Light of Regeneration, 21 March), when day and night are of equal length but the sun is beginning to grow in strength.

Arianrhod then proclaims that Lleu shall never have a wife born of woman. However Gwydion and Math use their magic to create a wife for Lleu from flowers of oak, broom and meadowsweet. They name her Blodeuwedd, meaning Flower-face. This takes us to *Calan Mai* (Irish *Beltaine*, May Day, 1 May), when young maidens are traditionally bedecked with flowers and choose young men to companion them in May Day revels.

Lleu is given a piece of land on which to set up his court. This takes us to *Alban Hefin*, the Light of Summer, Midsummer, when the sun is at its height and the god reaches the height of his powers, reigning over the land in glory. The wedding of Lleu and Blodeuwedd is appropriate to the next festival in the cycle, *Gwyl Awst* (Irish *Lughnasad*, Lammas, 1 August), the traditional time for the celebration of marriages or handfastings in Celtic countries.

One day, while Lleu is absent, Blodeuwedd invites a huntsman, Goronwy, to her castle where they feast and then sleep together. This takes us to the harvest festival of *Alban Elfed*, the Light of Autumn, 21 September, the Autumn Equinox), when day and night are again of equal length, but the sun's power begins to wane towards Midwinter.

Blodeuwedd and Goronwy conspire to kill Lleu with a

magical spear. This brings us to *Nos Galan Gaeaf*, the Nights of Winter Calends, Hallowe'en (Irish *Samhain*, 31 October), when the gates between this world and the realm of the ancestral spirits stand open, and the souls of the dead ride the night with the Wild Huntsman and his pack of hounds. The reign of the sun god ends and that of the dark god of winter begins.

As Lleu dies, his spirit leaves his body in the form of an eagle, ancient symbol of sovereignty. The eagle rests in an oak tree where it is found by Gwydion who is led to the spot by a sow. The sow represents the goddess in her dark, winter aspect. Gwydion charms the eagle down from the oak with a spell, which demonstrates the use of poetry as a magical ritual tool:

> Oak that grows between two plains;
> Darkened is the sky and hill.
> Shall I not know him by his wounds,
> That this is Lleu?

> Oak that grows in an upland plain,
> Is it not wetted by the rain? Has it not been drenched
> By nine score tempests?
> It bears in its branches Lleu Llaw Gyffes.

> Oak that grows beneath the steep;
> Stately and majestic its aspect.
> Shall I not address it thus,
> That Lleu may come to my lap?

When the eagle descends from the tree, Gwydion strikes it with his staff, restoring Lleu to human shape. This rebirth brings us back to Midwinter.

Gwydion and Lleu pursue Blodeuwedd into the mountains, where she is transformed into an owl by Gwydion. This event may have taken place at the festival of *Gwyl Forwyn* – folk festivities included a mock battle between the forces of Summer and Winter similar to that portrayed in the myth.

Goronwy is pursued to the banks of the river where Lleu himself had been slain. Goronwy shields himself with a standing stone, but Lleu casts his magic spear, piercing both the stone and Goronwy. This must have taken place at *Calan Mai*, the traditional end of winter.

A similar conflict between gods of summer and winter is mentioned in the Welsh tale of *Culhwch and Olwen*, where Creiddylad, 'Fresh Flowing', daughter of the god Lludd, is betrothed to Gwythyr, son of Greidawl ('Anger, son of Scorcher', an appropriate name for a fiery sun god). However, Gwynn ap Nudd ('White, son of Cloud, or Mist', clearly a winter god), carries Creiddylad away. King Arthur is called upon to make peace between them and gives judgement that the maiden should remain in her father's house, and that Gwynn and Gwythyr should fight for her every 1st of May until the day of doom, and that whichever of them should then be the victor should have the maiden.

The Greek myth of Persephone, also known as Kore, 'the Maiden', tells how she is taken by Hades, the dark Lord of the Underworld. This results in the death and decay of vegetation in the upper world until the god Hermes travels to the Underworld and persuades Hades to give up Persephone for part of the year. Her return to the upper world was celebrated annually in ancient Greece on 1 February. Her descent into the Underworld was re-enacted as part of the Greater Eleusian Mysteries over a nine-day period around the Autumn Equinox, when the harvest had been gathered in and new seed was being sown in the earth. Similar rites may well have been celebrated among the pagan Celts in honour of their own deities.

An Irish legend preserves what appears to be a ritual dialogue from just such a celebratory rite. The gods of Ireland, the *Tuatha de Danaan*, the 'Tribe of the goddess Dana', are feasting on the sacred hill of Tara when a young man comes to the door of the hall. The door-keeper challenges him, asking his name, and his profession, 'for no one is admitted here unless he is master of some craft'. Lugh explains that he is a carpenter, but the door-keeper dismisses this saying, 'We already have a very good one; his name is Luchtaine.'

The exchange continues, with Lugh stating that he is 'an excellent smith', 'a professional warrior', 'a harpist', 'a poet and storyteller', 'a Druid', 'a physician', 'a cup-bearer', and 'a worker in bronze'. The door-keeper replies that they already have someone within who has each of these skills. Lugh then tells him to ask the King 'if he has with him a man who is master of all these crafts at once, for, if he has, there is no need for me to come to Tara'. Lugh is invited in and hailed as *Ioldanach*, 'Master of All Arts'.

A similar ritual exchange occurs in the Welsh tale of *Culhwch and Olwen*. In this instance though, the court is not that of the gods, but of King Arthur, and the feast takes place on 1 January, the new year.

Such exchanges may have been part of ritual dramas performed at great public ceremonies. The modern concept of theatre originated in divine dramas staged at religious festivals in ancient Greece. Such performances were more than mere play-acting. The actors were seen as living embodiments of the gods and goddesses they portrayed, and as channels for their powers. The enactment of myth recreates it for the audience, renewing its spiritual power, reawakening the gods and restoring their energy to the land and people. Therein lies the true potency of the bardic tradition.

## Myths of Ireland:
### the Mythological Cycle

The traditional tales of Ireland are grouped into cycles dealing with the exploits of one or more central characters.

The Mythological Cycle is based around the collection of tales known as *Lebor Gabala Erinn*, The Book of the Taking of Ireland. It tells of five groups of invaders who came to Ireland prior to the current inhabitants, the Gaels. The first group dies in a flood except for the leader's consort, Fintan mac Bochra, 'White Fire son of Ocean', who lives on through all the subsequent invasions. Fintan changes shape, becoming in turn a salmon, an eagle, and a hawk. The salmon is a giver of wisdom, the eagle symbolic of sovereignty, the hawk of clarity of vision. Irish bards looked to Fintan as the supreme authority in matters of tradition. With his store of ancient knowledge, Fintan is an archetype of the Druid bard. A number of later Druids share his name, perhaps as reincarnations of his spirit.

The second group of invaders is led by Partholon. He and all his followers save Tuan mac Starn perish in a plague. Tuan also transforms into a stag, a wild boar, an eagle and a salmon. In salmon form he is caught and eaten by the wife of Cairell who later gives birth to him as Tuan son of Cairell.

The third invasion is led by Nemed. After many tribulations, his followers are forced to leave Ireland, but their descendants lead the next two invasions, the fourth group being the Fir Bolg, who appear to have been the earliest Celtic inhabitants of Ireland, and the fifth invasion bringing the *Tuatha de Danaan*, the 'Tribe of the goddess Dana', to Ireland. They are the gods of the Gaels, the second group of Celts to inhabit Ireland. The Gaelic gods include among their number the Dagda – or 'Good god', a sturdy, porridge-eating giant with a massive wooden club, a magical cauldron and a living harp carved from oak – referred to in one text as the god of Druidcraft. Other members of the *Tuatha* were the Morrigan, a fearsome battle-goddess, able to transform herself into raven, wolf, or snake; Nuada, the sword-wielding king of the gods; and Brighid, daughter of the Dagda.

The *Tuatha* defeat the Fir Bolg in a great battle, and in a second battle defeat the Fomoire, who seem to have been the gods of the Fir Bolg. This second battle, in which both sides invoke powerful magical forces, forms the climax of *Lebor Gabala Erinn*. The young sun god Lugh leads the *Tuatha* to victory, thereby clearing the way for the Gaels themselves to take possession of the country. After this the Fomoire and the For Bolg retire to the province of Connacht in the west of Ireland where they dwell still among the ancient stones and burial mounds that adorn its misty landscape.

## The Ulster Cycle

The Ulster Cycle centres around the great Irish hero, Cuchulainn, the 'Hound of Culainn'. The high point of the Cycle is the epic saga of the *Tain bo Cuailgne*, the 'Cattle Raid of Cooley'. This tells of Cuchulainn's single-handed defence of the province of Ulster against an army drawn from all the other Irish provinces. This army is led by a warrior queen, Maeve of Connacht, who wants to capture the magical Brown Bull of Cooley. Cuchulainn is aided by his father, the god Lugh, and hindered by the battle-goddess, the Morrigan, whose sexual advances he has spurned. Cuchulainn is eventually killed but uses his belt to tie himself to a standing stone so that even in death he will not fall before his enemies. As he dies the Morrigan perches on his shoulder in the form of a carrion crow.

## The Fenian Cycle

The Fenian Cycle is centred around the legendary warrior chief, Finn mac Cool, 'White, son of Hazel', and his war-band, the Fianna, elite bodyguard of the High Kings of Ireland. As a youth Finn gains wisdom and clairvoyance by eating one of the Salmon of Wisdom that swim in the River Shannon. According to some versions, this particular salmon is called Fintan and is presumably an incarnation of the same Fintan mac Bochra mentioned previously, who had been in Ireland since before the Flood. The salmon is given to Finn by an elderly Druid, also called Finn or Finegas. The tales of Finn and the Fianna involve much magic and mystery, and constant traffic with the Otherworld and its inhabitants. Finn's son, Oisin, for example, is born of a goddess, Sadb, who is magically transformed into a fawn. Finn, like the British King Arthur, is said to be not dead but sleeping in a hidden cave surrounded by his warriors, awaiting the hour of his country's greatest need when he will rise again.

## The Historical Cycle

The Historical Cycle consists of stories concerning the High Kings of Ireland who ruled from the ancient sacred hill of Tara, men such as Conn of the Hundred Battles and Niall of the Nine Hostages. These tales, while not in quite the same wildly magical mould as those of the other Cycles, still have their moments of enchantment. For example, we are told how Niall obtains the High Kingship after embracing a hideous black hag, who asks him for a kiss in return for a drink at her well. On receiving his embrace, she is instantly transformed into the most beautiful woman in the world, and when Niall asks, 'Who art thou?', she replies, 'King of Tara, I am Sovereignty ... and your offspring shall rule over every clan.' This theme of the hag transformed into a beautiful maiden by the embrace of a future king occurs frequently in early Irish literature, as well as in later British and French ballads and romances.

Having briefly examined Irish myths, let us now cross the Irish Sea and take a look at the legends of Britain.

# The Mabinogion

In British storytelling tradition, there is a single source which towers above all others. This is the medieval Welsh collection known as *The Mabinogion*. Strictly speaking, the term *Mabinogion* applies only to the first four of the eleven tales commonly linked together under this heading. Indeed, the term itself is incorrect, deriving from an error made by Lady Charlotte Guest, the first person to publish a full English translation of the tales. A more correct rendering would be *Mabinogi*, meaning 'Youthful Tales', which could be equivalent to the Irish *Macgnimartha*, 'Youthful Exploits', or might indicate that they were tales told to the young, or tales from the youth of the world.

## The Four Branches

The four tales, often referred to as the Four Branches, which comprise the *Mabinogi* proper, are *Pwyll Lord of Dyfed*, *Branwen Daughter of Llyr*, *Manawyddan Son of Llyr*, and *Math Son of Mathonwy*.

In the first of these, Pwyll, ruler of the kingdom of Dyfed in South Wales, changes places with Arawn, Lord of the Underworld of Annwn, and fights a battle in his stead. Pwyll marries a woman called Rhiannon, a euphemised Celtic horse goddess and embodiment of sovereignty. They have a child, Pryderi, born on May Eve.

The second Branch tells how Branwen, daughter of the sea god Llyr, is wed to Matholwch, King of Ireland. Matholwch takes Branwen to Ireland, where he mistreats her. Her brother, the giant Bran the Blessed, wades across the Irish sea, towing a fleet of warships behind him. Branwen is rescued, but Bran is mortally wounded. Those who escape include Pryderi, the sea god Manawyddan and the bard Taliesin. They return to Wales and Bran asks that his head be cut off and buried in the White Mount, where the Tower of London now stands, to protect Britain from invasion. *Bran* means 'raven', and a flock of ravens are still kept in the Tower of London. Tradition has it that if the ravens should leave the Tower the country will fall to invasion.

In the third Branch, Manawyddan marries Rhiannon, thereby gaining sovereignty over Dyfed. The land then falls under a spell which causes all of its inhabitants and their houses to vanish, except the main characters in the tale. Rhiannon and her son Pryderi enter a magical *caer* or 'fortification', where they find a golden bowl. When they touch the bowl, both they and the *caer* disappear. Manawyddan restores Rhiannon, Pryderi and the land of Dyfed by capturing the wife of the enchanter who has caused their disappearance and threatening to hang her if he does not remove his spell.

The fourth Branch tells how the Druid enchanter Gwydion and his brother Gilfaethwy use magic arts to obtain from Pryderi the Otherworld pigs which the Lord of Annwn had sent to him. Pryderi pursues them across Wales until he is slain by Gwydion. Gilfaethwy rapes Goewin, the virgin footholder of Math, lord of Gwynedd in North Wales. Goewin tells Math what has happened and says that he should look for someone to take her place. Math chooses Arianrhod, and so begins the cycle outlined above, of Lleu Llaw Gyffes and his magical bride Blodeuwedd, at the end of which Lleu becomes lord of Gwynedd.

The other seven tales that make up *The Mabinogion* are known as the *Four Independent Native Tales*, and the *Three Romances*.

## The Independent Native Tales

The first of the *Independent Native Tales* is *The Dream of Macsen Wledig*, in which the 4th-century Roman emperor, Magnus Maximus, 'Macsen', pursues and marries a woman called Helen of the Hosts, whom he encounters in a dream. Helen may originally have been a pagan British goddess. Both she and Macsen were claimed as ancestors by various Welsh dynasties.

*The Story of Lludd and Llevelys* tells of two mythical brothers, rulers of Britain and France respectively, during whose time three plagues fall upon Britain. The first is caused by a strange race called the Coranians, the second by a conflict between two dragons, and the third by a powerful giant. Through the wise advice of his brother, Lludd defeats all three plagues.

*Culhwch and Olwen* is an archaic tale that tells how a fate is laid on the young Culhwch by his step-mother, that he will never have a wife unless it be Olwen, daughter of a fearsome, one-eyed giant, Yspaddaden Penkawr. Culhwch asks his cousin, King Arthur, to help him win Olwen. Culhwch and six knights find Yspaddaden's castle. Olwen comes to meet them, and 'four white trefoils sprung up wherever she trod. And therefore she was called Olwen, "White Track"'. Yspaddaden is wounded in the leg, chest, and eye, but agrees to part with his daughter if Culhwch can complete a number of tasks — one is to hunt down a huge wild boar, another to find a magical child, Mabon ap Modron, 'Child, son of

Mother'. Culhwch and his companions are led to Mabon by a salmon. Arthur's warriors attack the castle where Mabon is held and release him. They pursue the boar across Britain and it kills many knights before they catch it. They then return to Yspaddaden, laden with all the magical treasures he had asked Culhwch to obtain, and the giant finally gives up Olwen.

The last of the *Independent Native Tales* is *The Dream of Rhonabwy*, which tells how Rhonabwy and his companions seek shelter in a strange hall. The interior is dark and filthy, inhabited by a toothless crone. Rhonabwy sleeps on a yellow ox-hide on a raised dais for three nights and three days, during which time he has a vision of King Arthur playing *gwyddbwyll*, 'wooden wisdom', an ancient board game, with Owein, son of Urien Rheged. The game the two men play is mirrored by a conflict between Arthur's knights and a group of ravens belonging to Owein. The presence of ravens suggests that *gwyddbwyll* was the Welsh equivalent of an Irish board game called *brandub*, 'black raven'. Both games seem to have had ritual significance and may also have been used for divination. Other sources indicate that bull or ox-hides were wrapped around bards seeking oracular visions during sleep.

### The Three Romances

The first of the *Three Romances* is *The Lady of the Fountain*, an early Arthurian tale featuring Owein ap Urien. A knight named Cynon tells how a man takes him to a castle and directs him to go at daybreak to a grassy mound where he will find a black giant armed with a huge iron club and surrounded by animals. The giant directs Cynon to a magical fountain beneath a tree, where Cynon fills the silver bowl he finds there with water, throws it over a stone and a great storm erupts. When the storm abates, a black knight on a black horse appears, defeats Cynon, and sends him back the way he came. Owein repeats Cynon's adventure except that he defeats the black knight and pursues him to a great city. The black knight, who is the lord of the city, dies, and Owein sees his widow, the Lady of the Fountain, mourning her loss and instantly falls in love with her. He marries her and takes the place of the black knight, defending the fountain which marks the border of her realm. After a while he returns to Arthur's court promising to come back to the Lady, but forgets to do so. When he finally recalls his promise he flees into the forest in shame and lives among wild animals, passing through further conflicts and adventures before eventually winning her back and returning with her to Arthur's court.

The romance of *Peredur son of Efrawg* is a kind of Celtic *Don Quixote*, dealing with the adventures of an innocent abroad. Peredur has been raised with no knowledge of weapons, horsemanship or other knightly skills, but takes himself to King Arthur's court to be ordained a knight. Arthur's knights make fun of him. Cei, one of Arthur's men, sends him out to fight a knight who has insulted Gwenhwyfar, Arthur's wife, promising that if Peredur wins he will be ordained a knight. He does win but refuses to enter the court until he avenges the blows Cei struck at two dwarfs who had greeted Peredur kindly. Peredur defeats many other knights in Arthur's name before arriving at the court of nine witches who teach him skill with weapons and horses. Peredur fights and defeats Cei and returns to Arthur's court. There, he falls in love with Angharad Golden-hand, who fails to return his love. He vows that he will not speak until she comes to love him and he rides out from the court again. On his return from his adventures he wins the love of Angharad. One day, while hunting a stag in the forest, Peredur comes to a hall where he encounters a one-eyed giant whose other eye was lost fighting a black serpent that lives in a barrow mound. Peredur sets out for the mound and slays the serpent, stopping off on the way at another castle of women who have a magic cauldron from which the dead emerge alive and killing a monster called Addanc which dwells in a cave with a standing stone at its entrance. Peredur returns once more to Arthur's court, where a hideous hag comes to him and sets him off on yet another adventure, to seek out a Castle of Wonders where he will gain wisdom. The tale ends with Peredur slaying the nine witches who had previously been his teachers.

The third romance, that of *Gereint son of Erbin*, tells how Arthur and his knights hunt a white stag. Gereint and Gwenhwyfar are left behind and see a woman on a white horse accompanied by a giant knight and a dwarf. Gereint follows the odd trio and reaches a castle where he is shown hospitality by an old couple and their beautiful daughter, Enid. The old man arms Gereint, who defeats the giant. Gereint marries Enid but comes to believe, quite wrongly, that she loves another. The two set out on horseback. Gereint orders her to be silent but each time she hears knights plotting to attack him she breaks her silence to warn him. He slays several groups of knights, receiving many wounds himself. He then fights three giants, the third striking him a blow which opens up all his previous wounds. He is carried, apparently dying, to a castle. The lord of the castle strikes Enid, causing her to cry out. At this, Gereint realises that Enid truly loves him and rises up, killing the lord and terrifying the rest of the castle's inhabitants who think he has risen from the dead. Gereint is healed, but hears of a 'hedge of mist' within which enchanted games are held and from which none have ever returned. Riding into the mist, he finds himself in an orchard where a hunting-horn hangs from an apple tree. Gereint defeats the chieftan, who tells him to sound the hunting-horn and when he does so the mist disperses and he is reunited with Enid. They return to his lands in Cornwall, where Gereint rules prosperously for the rest of his days.

## The Story of Taliesin

Another Welsh legend, the mysterious *Hanes* ('Story of') *Taliesin*, tells how the goddess Ceridwen has a husband called Tegid Foel, 'Beautiful Bald One', and three children: Morfran, 'Cormorant', Creirwy, 'Jewel Egg' and Afagddu, 'Utter Darkness'. Afagddu is so ugly that Ceridwen decides to make him wise to compensate for his looks. She brews a magic cauldron that has to boil for a year and a day. While she gathers herbs for the brew, she leaves an old man called Morda and a child named Gwion Bach, 'Little Innocent', looking after the cauldron. Three drops of the potion splash on to Gwion's hand and he puts it to his mouth, gaining the gifts of poetry, prophecy and shape-shifting. The rest of the brew is rendered not only useless but poisonous and the cauldron bursts. On her return, Ceridwen flies into a rage, pursuing Gwion through a series of animal transformations. Eventually, Gwion becomes a grain of wheat and is eaten by Ceridwen in the shape of a black hen. Nine months later she gives birth, ties the baby up in a leather bag, and casts him into the sea, where he is found by a prince. It is remarked that the baby has a radiant brow, hence he is called Taliesin, 'radiant brow'. The infant immediately composes his first poem and soon becomes Primary Chief Bard, first to the Court of Elphin, and then to the whole of Britain. This tale may be read as a series of initiations as bard, ovate and Druid.

## Arthur, Merlin and the
## Matter of Britain

Another major category of British bardic tales is the *Matter of Britain*, the stories of King Arthur and his knights. Arthur may have been an historical warlord in western Britain in the 6th century CE, who fought successfully against Saxon invaders who had gained control of southern and eastern England at that time. The oldest tales concerning Arthur are contained in *The Mabinogion* and in early British bardic poetry. Most of the surviving tales are much later, having been concocted by medieval writers such as Geoffrey of Monmouth, whose 12th-century *History of the Kings of Britain* is the principal source of medieval Arthurian myth. Geoffrey's *History* includes the story of how Merlin brings a stone circle, called the Giants' Ring-Dance, from Ireland and has it set up on Salisbury Plain, where it is now known as Stonehenge.

Merlin is adviser to Arthur's father, Uther Pendragon, and uses his magic power to enable Uther to sleep with Arthur's mother, Ygrain, by making him appear to her in the shape of her husband. The young Arthur becomes king by pulling a sword from a stone. The magical sword, Excalibur, is given to him by the Lady of the Lake who seems to be another incarnation of the goddess of Sovereignty. Arthur marries Guinevere, the Gwenhwyfar of *The Mabinogion* romances, and brings together the Knights of the Round Table, the Arthurian equivalent of Finn mac Cool's war-band, the Fianna.

### Gawain and the Greene Knight

Many legends surround individual Knights of the Round Table, one of the most interesting being the 14th-century poem *Sir Gawain and the Greene Knight*. This begins with Arthur and his knights celebrating Christmas and the New Year at the Court of Camelot. Their feasting is interrupted by the arrival of a huge, green-skinned man holding an axe. The Greene Knight challenges the assembled knights to strike his neck with his own axe, with the proviso that he be allowed to strike a blow in return after a year and a day. Gawain accepts the challenge and strikes off the Knight's head. The Greene Knight, however, picks up his severed head which tells Gawain to seek out the Green Chapel after a year and a day to receive the return stroke. The Knight then mounts his green horse and gallops out of the hall.

Gawain journeys in search of the Green Chapel and stays at a castle whose Lord goes out hunting each day, telling Gawain that they must give each other whatever they receive during the day. While her husband hunts game, the Lady hunts Gawain. He reluctantly receives her kisses and later passes them on to her husband in return for his day's catch. On the third day, however, the Lady gives Gawain her green silk belt and this he fails to pass on to the Lord, knowing that he will recognise it. When the time comes, Gawain keeps his appointment at the Green Chapel – a hollow mound beside a stream in a woodland glade. There he meets his opponent and stands to receive the axe stroke which cuts him only slightly. He then learns that, had he given the Lady's belt to his host, he would have received no hurt at all, for the Greene Knight is none other than the Lord, and he and his wife have been testing Gawain. Gawain returns to Camelot wearing the green belt as a symbol of his shame at having deceived his host, but Arthur's knights and their ladies think his adventure so worthy that they decide all Knights of the Round Table should henceforth wear a green belt.

An important theme in Arthurian myth is the quest for the Holy Grail, supposedly the chalice from which Jesus and his disciples drank at the last supper and/or the cup in which Christ's blood was caught when he was pierced by a spear as he hung on the cross. The Grail, though ostensibly a Christian symbol, can be seen as a version of the magic cauldron of pagan legend. Both Grail and cauldron have healing powers, both have strong feminine associations, and both grant wisdom and inspiration.

The *Matter of Britain* ends with Arthur mortally wounded at the Battle of Camlann and sending Sir Bedivere to cast the sword Excalibur back into the lake from whence it came. Arthur is then borne away to the mystical Isle of Avalon, 'Apple-Land', thought by some to be Glastonbury Tor in Somerset. Arthur does not die, however, but sleeps, awaiting the time when his country will have need of him once more. Thus is he known as *Rex Quondam Futurum*, 'the Once and Future King'.

Arthurian legend has inspired generations of creative artists, from the 15th-century poet Sir Thomas Malory, whose epic *Morte d'Arthur* is one of the great classics of English literature, through the artists of the 19th-century Pre-Raphaelite Brotherhood, to the film director John Boorman, whose *Excalibur* represents the most successful 20th-century version of the *Matter of Britain*.

## The World of Legend

Though the focus here has been on Celtic tales, every culture has its own myths and legends which perform similar functions and contain similar motifs. The non-Celtic bard should not have to look too far to find the traditional tales of her own culture, whether it be the Norse legends of Odin, Thor and Freya, the Greek myths of Zeus, Hera and the Olympian gods, their Roman equivalents, Jupiter, Minerva et al, the Hindu gods of the *Vedas*, Brahma, Agni, Sarasvati, Shiva, the Lakota tales of White Buffalo Woman, the African Fang people and their stories of the sky father, Nzame, and the forest mother, Nyule, or the Buryats of Siberia with their tales of the great bull prince, Buxa Noyon, and the cow mother, Buxtan Xatun.

Many of the cultures referred to here also have, or once had, their own specialists in the transmission of traditional songs and stories. The Greek epics, the *Iliad* and the *Odyssey*, were attributed to Homer, a Greek bard who lived around 700 BCE. The Brahmans of Vedic India were priests who sang hymns in praise of the gods and whose task it was to preserve and pass on those hymns for future generations. The verses which told of the exploits of Odin and his kin were the province of the *skald*, the Norse equivalent of the Celtic bard, while the songs of Charlemagne and his knights were passed on by the medieval French *trouvere*, or *troubadour*.

Knowing the traditional tales of our culture can lead to a deeper understanding of who we are, where we come from, and how we relate to our own and other cultures. This, in turn, helps us to relate to our ancestors, both human and divine. Discovering the traditional tales of other cultures can also teach us how much people all over the world have in common. Wherever we look, fundamental themes are repeated: light and dark gods struggle against each other, mortal heroes stand against overwhelming odds, helped or hindered by the gods, gods and mortals live, love, and die; and magicians, priests, Druids, shamans, wise women, or medicine men strive to wrest knowledge and power from the Otherworld. The fascination of such universal themes ensures that traditional tales continue to exert a timeless magic on the human mind. The current resurgence of interest in the bardic tradition will hopefully ensure that they are well performed and passed on to future generations.

But why leave it to others to carry the tradition? Become a bard yourself. Find some poems to recite, songs to sing or stories to tell. Several books of British and Irish poetry, songs and myths are listed in the Further Reading section; for those of other cultures, try your local library. Or make your own. Several cassettes are also listed in the Further Reading section, and these demonstrate many of the skills necessary to convey a poem, song or tale clearly and movingly, but actually seeing a good bard in action is the best way to learn. The movements and gestures, the look in the eye, the direct interaction with the audience, are vital to the art.

Having found the sources and studied the technique, practise. Share poems, songs and stories with your family and friends. This will help you to find material that works for you. You may find songs you absolutely love but can't quite put across, or you may find that stories you didn't think all that wonderful communicate beautifully to an audience. The only way to find out is by trial and error.

Another factor necessary to be a bard is perfect trust in the spirit of the material. Recognise that the poem wants to be heard, the song sung, the story told, that the characters within them want to come to life through your performance so that your audience will know and feel what they have known and felt. The material has a life of its own, you are merely its means of transmission. Traditional songs and tales have often been passed down over many generations. Be aware of the line of bards who have sung the songs and told the tales before you. When the spirit of a story takes you, you may sense the presence of the previous tellers standing behind you, urging you on. You may hear their voices adding extra phrases or incidents to the tale or reminding you of ones you had forgotten. Then you will know that you have been accepted by the tradition, and that this aspect of the way of the bard has truly opened to you.

In our electronic culture we have come close to losing the art of storytelling, except to our children at bedtime, forgetting that adults too respond to a well-told tale with a warmth, depth of emotion and intimacy that the television screen simply cannot match. There is an undeniable magic to sitting spellbound around a late-night camp-fire, or in a Gorsedd circle by the light of day, as a true exponent of the way of the bard paces the floor, unravelling some ancient tale of wonder, of dragons or witches, giants or Faery Folk, brave heroes and beautiful maidens, or of the creation of the world. At such times I realise that the bardic art will never die, for it carries with it a potency as old as the hills, a charm as fresh as spring water.

# Part III

# Healing and Awareness: The Path of the Ovate

# 5

# Divination

We now embark upon the path of the ovate, a path that leads from communication into understanding. One of the compasses we will use to navigate that path is divination, literally the art of communicating with the divine and finding the will of the gods. If you do not believe in a god or gods, you may think of it as a means of discovering the ways of fate. If you do not believe in fate, you may see it as a means of accessing your subconscious mind. Whatever your world view, divination provides a means to access otherwise hidden information in order to learn about ourselves and the world, to act wisely and live more effectively.

Our ancestors believed that the patterns of our lives are mirrored in the stars and other natural phenomena, and that our destiny is controlled by fate, whether seen as an abstract power or the will of the gods. In the 18th and 19th centuries, the growth of scientific rationalism produced a mechanical, deterministic model of the universe. This saw life as an interplay of natural forces that science would one day both explain and give us control over. In the 20th century, chaos theory has done much to restore the pagan idea that our lives are inextricably linked with the ebb and flow of seemingly random forces. Through divination we seek to understand the patterns of our lives, often through observing random patterns such as the fall of a coin or card, the flight of birds, or a face in the clouds.

The methods of divination used by Druids are many and varied, some ancient, some modern. Understood in its literal sense as communication with the divine, divination should be approached with the same reverence as prayer or ritual, otherwise it loses its meaning and becomes mere fortune-telling. Before undertaking divination you may like to burn incense, perhaps cast a circle. Certainly you should ask your ancestors, gods and guides for their help and guidance.

## Signs and Omens

Seeking signs and omens in natural phenomena such as clouds, water, fire, the movement of birds and animals, the shapes of trees and rocks, and the patterns of the stars is a method of divination that is probably as old as humankind. In the Highlands and Islands of Scotland, where augury from nature was once common, it is called *frith* and those who practise it are *fritheir*. Sometimes the talent is inherited, those who possess it being called *Clann an Fhritheir*, the Clan of the Seer.

In Scotland, *frith* is traditionally performed before sunrise on the first Monday after each quarter-day and accompanied by fasting, prayer and meditation on the subject about which information is being sought. Some say that the *fritheir* should be barefoot and bareheaded, some that he should walk three times around his hearthfire. With closed or blindfolded eyes, he goes to the door of his house, opens it and places a hand on either doorjamb. He then makes a final prayer to the all-seeing god for clarity of vision and understanding, opens his eyes and stares straight in front of him, taking careful note of whatever he should happen to see. If further information is needed the *fritheir* may circle his house once, sunwise, keeping his gaze fixed straight in front and again taking note of everything he sees.

With the technique, instructions are handed down as to what sights are lucky (*rathadach*) or unlucky (*rosadach*). To see a brown-skinned man is a good omen; a man coming towards the seer or looking towards him is even better, a man moving or turning away is bad. A man or animal in the process of standing up shows that the one enquired about is casting off the problem or illness that had afflicted them; if they are lying down the illness will continue. The sight of a woman is good, unless she is going away from the seer. To see a dog, horse, foal, calf or lamb facing the seer is lucky, to see a sheep especially so if the query is to do with a journey; to see a duck means good luck for seafarers.

Bad luck is presaged by most members of the crow family, particularly if moving towards the seer. A pig with its back to the seer is a bad sign, as are cats, unless you are on good terms with witches or are a member of one of the Cat Clans, i.e. the Mackintoshes or Macphersons. A goat is a bad omen for a journey.

Scottish tradition holds that it is more difficult to perform the *frith* across water, particularly across the sea, the reason being that the spirits who inhabit water are more able and willing than those of land to confuse the sight of the seer.

## The Language of Birds

Many forms of divination are variants of *frith*, with more or less ceremony attached. Classical writers comment on the

Gauls divining from the behaviour or speech of crows, while a medieval Irish manuscript sets out precise meanings to be drawn from the behaviour of ravens and wrens. A raven calling from above an enclosed bed in a house is said to predict the arrival of a distinguished grey-haired guest or clergymen. If a lay cleric, the raven calls 'bacach', if he is in holy orders, the raven says 'gradh gradh'. If it calls 'grob grob' or 'gracc gracc' then bardic satirists or warriors are coming. If a raven goes before you on a journey, this is a good sign; if it approaches from the left, this means an argument. If a wren calls from the north-east, a woman, either alone or with a companion, is coming to see you; if it calls from the east, bards are coming, or news of them, if from the west, expect an unwanted visit from a relative. If it sings from a standing stone, the death of a great man is signalled.

Divination by magpies survives in the popular child's rhyme:

> *One for sorrow,*
> *two for joy,*
> *three for a girl*
> *and four for a boy,*
> *five for silver,*
> *six for gold,*
> *seven for a secret*
> *never to be told,*
> *eight for a wish,*
> *nine for a kiss,*
> *ten for a marriage*
> *never to be old.*

Such specifics are entertaining but may not be particularly useful. Rather than holding the mind to a rigid set of meanings, it may be better just to be aware of traditional associations with plants, trees and animals.

In ancient Ireland specialist diviners called *Neladoir*, 'cloud-watchers', divined the answers to questions put to them by studying the shifting patterns and images in cloud formations. Most of us will at some time have stared into a fire and seen shapes in the flames. With focused intention, this too can be a means of divination.

A vision in a woodland glade a few years ago revealed to me a variation on the *frith* technique. When seeking an omen, hold your hands out in front of you at eye level, palms facing away from you, fingers pointing upward, index fingers and thumbs touching, thumbs pointing downward. This produces a tear-drop shaped aperture that frames a small section of the world, helping to keep the attention fixed. For those who find vision-seeking difficult, it has the added advantage that the eyes will sometimes focus at the range of the hands, sometimes on the world beyond. This focusing and defocusing can help the mind to recognise shapes and patterns that might otherwise be missed.

## Ogham: *the Secret Language*

Another method of divination with a long history behind it uses an alphabet called Ogham. This originally consisted of 20 letters, to which a further five were added later. The original 20 letters each consist of between one to five straight lines or notches intersecting a stem line. The earliest surviving Ogham inscriptions are carved on standing stones, with the edge of the stone forming the stem line. Inscriptions are usually written from the base of the stone upwards, sometimes passing over the top and continuing down the other side. However, Ogham is impractical for writing much more than short inscriptions. It seems to have been invented in Ireland, probably in the 2nd century CE, and developed into a complex system in which each letter had many possible meanings, being used in magic, divination and, perhaps, as an early form of musical notation.

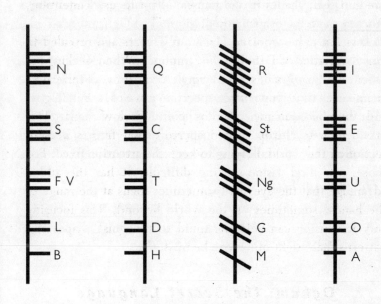

The Ogham alphabet

The Ogham alphabet is sometimes called Beth-Luis-Nion – the Gaelic names of the first three letters, which are also the names of trees; Beth is the birch, Luis the rowan or mountain-ash, and Nion the ash tree. However, before the first stone inscriptions were carved, the N and V were transposed, so that the final order of the letters became:

B L V (or F) S N, H D T C Q, M G NG Z R, A O U E I

The name Ogham was also applied to secret languages and cyphers used among initiates of Irish bardic colleges. Ogham speech was not a true language but consisted of ordinary Irish words disguised in various ways, such as by adding letters or syllables, changing initial letters, or reversing whole words.

Below are the Ogham letters with their tree names in Irish and English. The fourth column includes suggested equivalents for use in an English version of the spoken Ogham back-slang, inspired by the work of Dylan ap Thuin, Archdruid of the Insular Order of Druids. The simplest method of creating a spoken Ogham is to select a single tree name and insert the name each time it appears in speech in place of its initial letter. For example, using the word sallow in place of the letter 's', the phrase, 'Listen, I must say something,' becomes 'Lisallowten, I musallowt salloway sallowomething.'

## *The Ogham Letters*

| Letter | Irish | English | Ogham back-slang |
|---|---|---|---|
| The 'B' group | | | |
| B | beith | birch | birch |
| L | luis | rowan | larch |
| F | fearn | alder | fir or fern |
| S | saille | willow | sallow |
| N | nion | ash | nut or nettle |
| | | | |
| The 'H' group | | | |
| H | huath | hawthorn | hawthorn |
| D | duir | oak | durmast |
| T | tinne | holly | trefoil |
| C | coll | hazel | cedar or crab apple, depending on whether the 'c' is soft or hard |
| Q | quert | apple | quince |
| | | | |
| The 'M' group | | | |
| M | muin | vine | mistletoe |
| G | gort | ivy | gorse |
| Ng | ngetal | broom or reed | – |

| St | straif | blackthorn | – |
|----|--------|------------|---|
| R | ruis | elder | rowan |

*The 'A' group*

| A | ailm | silver fir | apple or ash |
|---|------|------------|--------------|
| O | onn | furze | oak |
| U | ura | heather | ulmus |
| E | eadha | aspen | elder |
| I | idho | yew | ivy |

*Diphthongs*

| Ea | ebad | eclampsia or aspen | – |
|----|------|--------------------|---|
| Oi | oir | spindle tree | – |
| Ui | uillean | ivy, woodbine or honeysuckle | – |
| Io | pin | pine or gooseberry | – |
| Ae | emancoll | witch hazel | – |

As some English letters and sounds aren't represented in the Ogham alphabet, the following could be added for the purposes of the back-slang:

| | |
|---|---|
| J [juniper] | W [willow, or witchhazel] |
| K [kelp] | X [xylem] |
| P [pine] | Y [yew] |
| Th [thorn] | Z [zinnia] |
| V [vine] | |

## Ogham Divination

An Irish legend, 'the Wooing of Etain', tells of a Druid named Dalan using Ogham divination to find where the god Midir had taken Etain. He cut four wands of yew on which he inscribed three Oghams, and used them to find the *eochra ecsi*, 'keys of knowledge'. These showed him that she had been taken to the Faery mound of Breg Leith.

Other Irish sources refer to the use in divination of four Ogham-inscribed yew wands called *fews*. The number four may relate to the division of Ogham letters into four groups. If the *fews* each had five sides, one of the 20 Ogham characters could be cut on to each angle. The Ogham to be read would then be the one uppermost when the *few* is cast.

A method of Ogham divination favoured by some modern-day Druids uses 20 *fews* made from the wood of each of the 20 letter trees, each *few* having its letter cut on it. The *fews* are usually quite small, perhaps three or four inches long, and are placed in a bag, often of leather. The diviner pulls out one or more *fews* at random, usually no more than three, and reads the answer to her question in them. Some cast the *fews* on to a cloth, reading information from the way they fall in relation to each other; some use a cloth decorated with a pattern called Fionn's Window, one of several arrangements

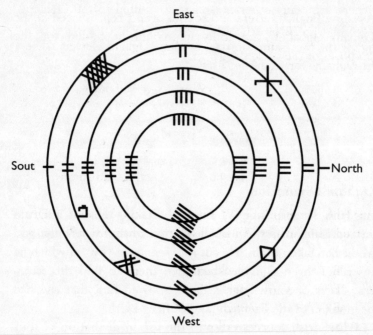

Fionn's Window

of Oghams found in *The Scholar's Primer*, a textbook of the
bardic colleges of medieval Ireland. This increases the range
of possible readings by combining the letters on the *fews* with
those marked on the cloth.

The Roman historian Tacitus describes a similar method of
divination in use in Germany in the 1st century CE. A branch
of a nut-bearing tree was sliced into strips. These were
marked with signs and thrown at random on to a white cloth.
A priest or the head of the family then offered a prayer to the
gods and, looking up at the sky, picked up three strips, one at
a time, reading their meaning from the signs cut on them.

Meanings attributed to the Ogham alphabet are set out in
*The Scholar's Primer*. It includes the following list of phrases
linked with the letters of the Ogham alphabet.

There are many other meanings attributed to the Ogham
letters in *The Scholar's Primer*, based on lists of words beginning with the same initial as the Ogham letter. The
bird-Ogham, for example, lists:

| B | besan | pheasant |
| L | lachu | duck |
| F (V) | faelinn | gull |
| S | seg | hawk |
| N | naescu | snipe, and so on |

Using the same principle, English-speaking Druids might
construct similar lists. An English bird-Ogham might begin:

| B | blackbird |
| L | lark |
| F (V) | finch |
| S | swallow |
| N | nightingale, and so on |

## Phrases Linked with the Ogham Alphabet

| Letter | Irish | English | Phrase 1 | Phrase 2 |
|--------|-------|---------|----------|----------|
| **The 'B' group** | | | | |
| B | beith | birch | faded trunk and fair hair | most silvery of skin |
| L | luis | rowan | delight of eye | friend of cattle |
| F | feam | alder | shield of warrior-bands | guarding of milk |
| S | saille | willow | hue of the lifeless | activity of bees |
| N | nion | ash | checking of peace | fight of women |
| **The 'H' group** | | | | |
| H | huath | hawthorn | pack of wolves | blanching of face |
| D | duir | oak | highest of bushes | carpenter's work |
| T | tinne | holly | a third or a good portion | fires of coal |
| C | coll | hazel | fairest of trees | friend of cracking |
| Q | quert | apple | shelter of a hind | force of the man |
| **The 'M' group** | | | | |
| M | muin | vine | strongest of effort | condition of slaughter |
| G | gort | ivy | sweeter than grasses | abundance of mead |
| Ng | ngetal | broom or reed | a physician's strength | – |
| St | straif | blackthorn | strongest of red | increasing of secrets |
| R | ruis | elder | intensest of blushes | redness of faces |
| **The 'A' group** | | | | |
| A | ailm | silver fir | loudest of groanings | beginning of an answer |
| O | onn | furze | helper of horses | smoothest of work |
| U | ura | heather | in cold dwellings | growing of plants |
| E | eadha | aspen | distinguished wood | synonym for a friend |
| I | idho | yew | oldest of woods | most withered of wood |

Other divinatory techniques used by modern Druids include card sets such as my own *Druid Tarot*, Liz and Colin Murray's *Celtic Tree Oracle*, or Philip and Stephanie Carr-Gomm's *Druid Animal Oracle*. Others use Archie Fire Lame Deer's *Lakota Sweat Lodge Cards*, or Jamie Sams' *Medicine Cards*, seeing similarities between Native American spirituality and that of our pagan European ancestors. Others use the tarot, runes, astrology or the *I Ching*. Let personal inspiration guide you to which method suits you best.

Through exploring the bardic path, we open ourselves to the flow of Awen, learning to recognise its presence and channelling it into creativity. The path of the ovate leads to a new understanding of Awen, now seen as a conduit for information from the Otherworld. The 12th-century writer, Gerald of Wales, wrote of a group of diviners operating in his day called *Awenyddion*, 'Awen-inspired Ones', who went into a trance state in which they gave prophecies in verse. Through divinatory techniques such as those outlined above, we attune ourselves to receive messages from this world and the worlds beyond. With continued practice, we begin to shift our consciousness into a deeper understanding of the Otherworld, the world of spirit, and how it interacts with our own.

## Second Sight

This process of attunement can awaken us to direct visionary experience of the Otherworld, traditionally referred to as second sight. It not only enables us to catch glimpses of distant or future events, but also to see Otherworld inhabitants such as tree spirits and the Faery Folk. The reality or otherwise of such beings has been the subject of much debate. In Druidry, those who remain undecided are encouraged to accept their existence as a catma (see Introduction), behaving *as if* they are objectively real and treating them with due respect. Given the tricks some Otherworld inhabitants are wont to play on unwary mortals, this is sound common sense!

The Otherworld exists alongside our own. It is often described as being hidden from our world by a veil of mist. For those gifted with second sight, this mist disperses and the spirits of nature, the Faery Folk and their kin are seen clearly. One of the defining abilities of the Druid, as we shall see in Chapter 8, is the ability to walk between the worlds. In order to do so without stumbling it is necessary to be able to see those other worlds. The path of the ovate includes the development of that sight.

Second sight requires a shift in consciousness. Some are born with this ability, others develop it naturally as they grow, some work hard over many years to achieve it, and some never possess it. The first requirement is to acknowledge that other worlds exist. The second I can best describe as a kind of defocusing on the mundane world that allows sight of the Otherworld to come through. You may find that the defocusing technique described on page 90 helps. As with many other talents, the way to develop it is either through good teaching or through practice, preferably both. Those who journey between the worlds can act as guides, taking you on such a journey to awaken you to the sight of the spirit world, and to awaken the spirit world to you.

Don't be in too much of a hurry though, for second sight may bring visions of ugliness as well as beauty, of death as well as life. For this reason, many of those born with the sight regard it as a curse rather than a blessing. Learning to deal with both the darkness and the light is a vital part of the ovate path. Look again at the turning of the wheel of the year as set out in Chapter 2. When you cast your circle walk it from North to North, from the dark womb of Midwinter through the growth of Springtime, the vigour of summer and finally back to the womb of winter. This is the path of the ovate; the path of fate and time. Studying the processes of birth, growth, death, decay and subsequent rebirth in the natural world, we come to understand the cycle of our lives. This is the primary study of the ovate.

# 6

# Healing

Healing within the Druid tradition operates through many levels of being. As the practice of Druidry becomes more ingrained in day to day living, it becomes clear that every aspect of the path impacts on our spiritual, psychological and physical well-being. At the soul level, we seek to respond to the deepest needs of the individual, working through the pain of past lives to bring about healing in the present, and reconnecting with our ancestors of blood and of spirit using ritual and meditation. At the physical level we use herbs, massage and other techniques. The practical work of this chapter includes ways of making contact with one's ancestors, and a journey in spirit to find one's place of healing.

Conventional medicine begins from the physical level. In Druidry, however, we address the individual first and foremost as a spiritual being. The concept is simple: the spiritual realm is seen as the origin of all other levels of being, so anything that has an effect in that realm naturally affects every other aspect of existence. The spiritual provides the blueprint from which emotion and intellect build the view of reality from which we construct our physical world, our environment, and our relationships. So, by working with the spirit, we bring about changes in the emotional, intellectual and physical worlds; in heart, mind and body.

## Journeys of the Soul

A tenet held by many Druids is that we live not one but many lives. Some hold that we live again and again in this world, others that we pass through death to new life in other worlds, yet most maintain that we grow in knowledge and experience through each of those lives. Some believe that we pass through many stages of being, experiencing the life of stone, grass, bee, tree, lizard, rabbit, raven, fish, deer, bear or other creature before or between our human lives; others believe that this cycle of birth, life, death and rebirth leads ultimately to a point of understanding at which we identify ourselves completely with the great powers of the universe, merging individual consciousness with the whole of creation.

As the soul passes from life to life, we learn. Sometimes we learn well, other lessons we forget in the space between lives or through the trauma of birth, or lose among the overwhelming sensations of childhood. The pain of past lives can remain with us and, if we don't acknowledge and free ourselves from it, we may be prevented from moving on. The exploration of past lives offers a path to healing and freedom. Reliving severe traumas of past lives can be equivalent to reliving those experiences in this life, and may best be done with the help and guidance of a trained counsellor. However, guidance and healing can equally be achieved through working with our ancestors of blood and spirit, our soul friends, gods and guides, who may have been with us during those previous lives.

In the first chapter of this book we journeyed through the history of the Druid tradition, seeking our vision of the archetypal Druid. Now let's take another journey, this time through our ancestral blood line, looking for blockages in the flow of spirit that may be caused by areas of trauma in our relationships with our ancestors. The process of healing the past began when we acknowledged and gave thanks for the gift of life bequeathed to us by our parents, grandparents and previous generations. The following exercise takes that initial healing further.

## THE ANCESTOR TREE

This exercise may be used to connect with our ancestors of spirit as well as those of blood.

☆ First, find a tree. Any tree might do, but try to find one that you feel a resonance with. You might feel drawn to the majesty and stability of the oak, the dark wisdom of the yew, the lively brightness of the rowan, the ethereal beauty of the silver birch. For more information on the meanings associated with trees, refer to Chapter 5. If you need to, ask for guidance from your gods and guides.

☆ When you have found your tree, pause when you reach the edge of the spread of its branches and ask the dryad, the spirit of the tree, to accept your presence and the work that you are about to do. Be open to the response you get. If you sense that the tree is unwilling to help you, bid it farewell and move on. If the tree is willing to accept you, move under its branches and sit with your back against the trunk. Take a few deep, slow breaths to regulate your breathing. If it seems appropriate, you might like to chant the Awen to awaken the flow of spirit.

☆ Be aware of your physical body. Feel its solid presence beneath the tree. Make sure that you are comfortable and well supported. Feel the tree against your back. It is your family tree. The trunk against which you rest is where you are now, with all the support and strength that you have around you. Its roots are your ancestors, its branches your descendants. Today we are going to journey into the roots.

☆ As in Chapter 1, the first step on the journey is to give thanks to your parents for the gift of life. Take this opportunity to heal any rifts between you and your parents, including any blocks of anger or mistrust that still exist between you. Explore the negative aspects of your relationship, then find the positive results they may have had in your life. Find what you have gained and give thanks.

☆ Now sense how the tree is rooted into the earth. You too are rooted in the earth through the bloodline of those whose genetic inheritance you carry. Become aware of your grandparents and explore your relationship with them, looking again for what their lives and their inheritance has given you. When you are ready, move your consciousness back to your great-grandparents and so on through the generations. There is no need to visit every generation. You may find that you skip some but are drawn towards others. Some you may briefly acknowledge as you pass, others you may wish to spend time with, absorbing what they have to say. Go back through as many or as few generations as you feel comfortable with. You can always go further another time.

☆ You may feel your consciousness sliding down the roots of your tree. If you do, go with this feeling, it is the way in which the spirit of the tree is responding to your journey. If you don't feel this, don't worry, the tree is still there supporting you.

☆ As you move back in time, be alert for any problems, tensions or blockages. When you find them, work through them as you did with your parents. Look for the roots of each problem and how it has affected subsequent generations. Then look beyond the problem to the positive results that may have flowed from it. Offer this positive input to refresh and purify your genetic stream.

☆ When you have journeyed as far as you wish to at this time, retrace your steps, giving thanks to each generation of your ancestors for the beneficial gifts they have passed down to you through your genetic line, that you may pass on to future generations. Where gifts are other than beneficial, work towards healing, not only on your own behalf but for your ancestors and for the generations yet unborn. Make prayers or offerings for healing if this seems appropriate.

☆ When you have moved back through the generations to your own parents, bring yourself back to the present by focusing on your breathing, becoming aware again of the physical reality of your body, feeling the earth beneath you and the firm presence of the tree at your back. Look around you. Take in the here and now.

☆ When you are ready, give thanks to the ancestors, to your gods and guides and to the spirit of the tree. You might like to make some small offering before you leave the place, perhaps of flowers, bread, mead or water. All these things will feed the tree and the creatures that live around it.

The performing of rituals, whether alone or in a group, is itself a healing process through the reconnection it offers with the spirits of the land, our ancestors, gods and guides, the cycles of our lives and of the world. Meditations also offer similar opportunities for reconnection.

## Herbs and Healing Gods

Druids use many other healing techniques, both traditional and modern. Among the traditional, herbalism is popular and widespread. The magical and medicinal use of plants fits well with the animistic vision of Druidry, that sees all things as sacred and imbued with spirit. Classical sources refer to Druids in Gaul using mistletoe medicinally, calling it 'all-heal'. Mistletoe was long used to treat epilepsy and other convulsive disorders and has also been used to stop internal bleeding. More recently it has been put forward as a treatment for some forms of cancer. Most plants have some medicinal properties.

An ancient Irish legend vividly portrays the Druidic approach to healing, combining magic with medicine. Diancecht was the medicine man of the old gods, the *Tuatha de Danann*. When their chief, Nuada, lost his hand in battle, it was Diancecht who made him a replacement of silver that was every bit as supple and strong as his hand of flesh had been. Diancecht had a son, Miacha, who inherited his father's healing skills. Indeed, some said he was a better healer than Diancecht. On hearing this, Nuada sent for the lad. Miacha asked where Nuada's severed hand was and, on hearing that it had been buried, he dug it up. He removed Nuada's silver hand and held the withered hand of flesh to the stump. As he did so, he uttered an incantation: 'Sinew to sinew and nerve to nerve be joined.' After three days and nights, the hand had grown back to the arm and was as good as ever.

When Diancecht heard of his son's work, he flew into a rage at having been outdone by a mere youth. He struck Miacha with his sword, cutting his skin. Miacha healed the wound instantly. Diancecht sliced him to the bone with his next blow, but again Miacha healed himself. The third blow clove through Miacha's skull and into the brain. Again the boy healed himself. His father then struck him a fourth time, cleaving his son's skull in two so that he finally died. Diancecht, appalled at what he had done, buried his son and on his grave there grew 365 healing herbs, each one a cure for a different ailment. Airmid, Miacha's sister, took each of these plants and laid them out on her cloak according to the ailments they would cure. Diancecht was furious at what she was doing in her brother's memory, angered that, if the secrets of these plants became known, no one would honour him for his healing gift any more. He took the cloak and shook it vigorously, scattering the plants in confusion. Had it not been for that act, so the story says, we should now have a cure for every illness and humankind would be immortal. Thanks to Diancecht's anger, subsequent generations have had to do what they can to rediscover the lore of herbs.

The story illustrates how our ancestors regarded the gods as having the ability to give or promote healing. Some were seen to have influence in particular areas. The Irish goddess Brighid, for example, is invoked in pregnancy for protection of the unborn child, in labour for a safe and speedy delivery, and for the protection of young children. The Romano-British god Nodens, equivalent to the Irish Nuada and Welsh Nudd, was invoked for the healing of wounds. Others, such as the goddess Sulis, patroness of the healing waters at Bath in Somerset, offered more general healing.

## Healing and the Faery Folk

A Welsh folktale tells how a poor farmer met a beautiful maiden who lived in a lake in the Black Mountains. She agreed to marry him and make him wealthy, on condition that he would not strike her three blows. He did indeed strike her three times, albeit by accident, and she returned to the lake. While they were together, she had borne the farmer three sons. The three went down to the lake shore, where their mother appeared, gave them a bag of medicines and told them that they would be great physicians and so would their children after them. Their fame spread and they and their descendants were known as the Physicians of Myddfai.

This is one of many examples of the Faery Folk helping humans to heal. Other Faery Folk brought healing stones, some of which have been preserved for many centuries by the families to which they were given.

Whenever we receive a gift from the spirit world, whether it be of teaching, wisdom, inspiration or, as in these tales, something more tangible, we should always give something in return. This may be an offering of bread, mead or flowers, a song or poem, an act of generosity towards someone, or a simple acknowledgement of the gift and honouring of the giver.

Other healing techniques employed by modern Druids include massage, aromatherapy, acupuncture and healing through spirit and sound. The common link is not so much the therapies themselves as the attitude of mind that the Druid brings to them. It is not the illness that is treated but the person with the illness. Each person is treated as an individual rather than a collection of symptoms. There is also a clear recognition that individuals should, as far as possible, be given full understanding of and responsibility for their own treatment.

## The Place of Healing

Each person has their own place of healing, either in this world or the Otherworld. It offers perfect peace and security and a spiritual centre from where healing can begin. Visiting the place of healing can bring specific guidance on how treatment should proceed; we may be shown what we need to restore spirit, mind and body to health and well-being.

The place of healing can be found through meditation, divination, or with the help of a spirit guide or someone experienced in guiding spirit journeys. It can emerge from a dream or may be found during waking life. For some it may be the white sand of a tropical beach, for others the secure darkness of a deep cave, a sunlit forest glade, a rock shelf behind a waterfall, a hollow on a mountainside, a mossy tree beside a woodland stream, the heat of the desert or an Arctic ice-flow. It may be a place you knew in childhood, an ancient sacred site, or some enchanted place that you may never have seen in this world.

Ask your guides to help you find your place of healing. I

cannot take you there through the pages of this book; it is too intimate, too personal to you. It is your place. Those who walk with you in spirit, whether in this world or the worlds beyond, may help you to find it. Then, when you are troubled in spirit, mind or body, you may go there. In the peace that you find there, you will be given what you need to restore you to health.

So may it be!

# Part IV

# Ritual and Change: The Path of the Druid

# 7

# Ritual

Ritual is the grammar that shapes and gives pattern and meaning to the language of our lives. Through ritual we express recognition and reverence for those things we hold sacred, and sanctify those things we hold dear. Ritual provides a focus for prayer and meditation, an avenue for healing, a vehicle for shifting between worlds.

In Druidry, we mark with ritual the passage of the sun through the seasons and the changes that flow through spring, summer, autumn and winter. For an understanding of the seasonal rites, see Chapter 2. Many Druids also honour the monthly course of the moon with rites, often at the full or new moons. The rituals of sun and moon are celebratory, honouring the natural world and the spirits of land, sea and sky, the gifts of creativity and inspiration, those present sharing poetry, music, songs and stories. The rituals include offerings of mead, wine, water or other drink in honour of the sky father whose rain fertilises the earth, and of bread or other food to the earth in honour of the nurturing mother who feeds us and to whose embrace we return when our time is done. Through these rites we attune ourselves with the natural processes of the world.

In industrialised nations many of us live lives largely divorced from the world of nature. We live in hermetically sealed homes, protected from seasonal variations in temperature by double-glazing, central heating and air conditioning. Most of us are urban dwellers, detached from the processes of food production, getting our food pre-packaged in supermarkets rather than directly from field or hedgerow as our ancestors did. Electric lighting lessens the impact of nightfall; street lighting obscures the stars. This is the life that many of us have chosen. And industrialisation does bring many benefits. I'm writing this on a word processor and I also like CD players, tape recorders, television and electronic music. However, when we lose touch with the natural world, we lose an intimacy of contact with the processes of birth, life, death and decay that shaped the world of our ancestors and inspired their spirits. We also lose contact with the spirits of nature that are a vital element of Druid tradition. In losing these things, we are cut off from potent sources of teaching, healing and inspiration. Through ritual we can reestablish our connections with our ancestors and the natural world.

Just as we make rites that mark the flow of the changing seasons of moon and sun, so we mark the flow of our lives with rites of passage that acknowledge and celebrate the changes that come with birth, puberty, commitment to a partner, menopause and death. Through ritual, we explore the meaning of these changes and the ways in which they affect our lives, preparing us for each new stage in life's journey. The construction and performance of such rituals is an important part of the work of the Druid.

Many rites have no set text, deriving from an immediate, spontaneous response to time, place, people and spirit. Others are more formal, especially where many of those taking part may be unused to the shape and nature of ritual. As Druid priests, we increasingly find ourselves called upon to make rites of passage with and for non-Druids. In such circumstances, we generally begin with a written script which will be adapted to fit specific needs. For example, when performing a Druid wedding we will speak with the couple beforehand to discuss what we and they will say and do during the rite, ensuring that its meaning is as deep and powerful as possible for them. Within the basic framework of Druid ritual we will work with their needs and expectations to ensure that their own gods and ancestors are appropriately honoured, their friends and relatives included, the site properly prepared, music provided, and so on.

## The Gorsedd Rite

The rite that follows includes many elements common to Druid ritual. It forms the basis of the open Gorsedd celebrations that take place under the aegis of the British Druid Order at each of the eight festivals of the year at sacred sites in Britain and overseas. The rite given below does not include specific seasonal elements as these will obviously change from festival to festival. Such seasonal elements often include the acting out of mythical dramas appropriate to the festival. See Chapters 2 and 4 for guidance.

The ritual was written and compiled by myself and Emma Restall Orr from historical sources, our own inspiration, and contributions from members of the Gorsedd. It is not to be taken as holy writ, but as a source of guidance and inspiration. The words spoken should reflect the spirit of the rite rather than slavishly follow the written text.

A Gorsedd is a gathering of bards. The term Gorsedd (literally 'high seat') originally referred to prehistoric sacred mounds, often with single trees growing on them, which were places of tribal assembly, festival celebration, law-giving and the inauguration of kings. In times past, sacred kings were ritually wedded at such sites to a representative of the female spirit of the land. At some point, the assemblies themselves came to be known as Gorseddau after the mounds on which they were held.

Our Gorseddau are open, multifaith celebrations at which folk of many spiritual traditions gather to honour their gods, the earth and each other. In this, they reflect another central tenet of Druidry: tolerance for the beliefs and practices of others. Within the Gorsedd circle we celebrate the turning of the year through the cycle of eight festivals recognised by many modern pagan traditions. We also celebrate rites of passage, offering Druid weddings or handfastings, blessings for children, croning, and remembrance of the dead. Most celebrations include initiations into the Gorsedd for those wishing to make a personal dedication to the spirit of the place, and to the way of the bard, which is to learn to express the spirit of inspiration through the creative arts. Bread and mead are blessed and shared during the rites, which also include eisteddfod sessions where bards are encouraged to offer stories, poetry, music, song or dance.

Before the ceremony begins, the priest and priestess invite people to participate in the ceremony as follows: a woman to represent the Guardian Spirit of the Place; three bards or musicians to assist in weaving the circle; four people, prefer-ably of different spiritual traditions, to make the calls to the four directions; a priest and priestess to help with the sharing of bread and mead.

Once everyone has assembled, the gathering forms two groups: one, the Goddess party, led by the representative of the Guardian Spirit of the Place, takes one course, while the other group, the God party led by the priest, takes another, processing sunwise to the point at which the two meet again to begin the rite.

**Priest:** Once again the Solar Wheel returns to [name of festival], and we come to this most sacred place and ask the Guardian Spirit of [name of place] to accept the gifts we bring and bless us as we enter in to celebrate the sanctity and beauty of our Mother Earth.

He presents a gift to the Guardian.

**Priest:** That which comes from the Earth, returns to the Earth.

**Guardian:** In the name of the Mother of All Living, the Guardian Spirit of [name of place], and the ancestors of our people, I accept the gifts you offer. All who come here are welcome, but thrice blessed are those who come with reverence and love.

> *The blessings of the goddess be with you,*
> *The blessings of the guardian be with you,*
> *The blessings of the ancestors be with you,*
>    *and with our children,*
> *With you and with our children.*
> *Enter now and welcome.*

Others may also present gifts to the Guardian and receive a blessing from her in return. Priest and priestess then lead the procession to the place where the Gorsedd circle is formed.

## *Opening the Circle*

The place where the rite is to occur is often prepared in advance, a circle marked out and cleared, perhaps decorated with seasonal flowers, an altar set up, candles, a water bowl and incense provided. The presiding priests may make a short purification ritual in the circle beforehand if this seems appropriate.

We begin by greeting the spirits of the land and of our ancestors, welcoming all who have come.

**Priestess:** Hail, O spirits of this place, you who are the embodiment of this sacred land on which we are gathered. As we honour you, so I ask that you accept our presence here. Hail, O ancestors, you who have walked these ways before us, you whose songs echo in the air around us, whose tears and laughter echo in our hearts. Hail to you, both seen and unseen, who gather here this day. Let all who come in peace be welcomed to our circle. Hail and welcome!

**All:** Hail and welcome!

**Priest:** We begin this celebration by calling for peace, that in peace the voice of spirit may be heard.

> *May there be peace in the east.*
> *May there be peace in the south.*
> *May there be peace in the west.*
> *May there be peace in the north.*
> *May there be peace throughout all the world.*
> *So may it be!*

**All:** So may it be!

**Priestess:** We gather here in peace to celebrate this Gorsedd of Bards of [name of place], and the festival of [name of festival], and the sanctity of our Mother Earth. Let us now weave our circle, that the spirits of those who are gathered here may be blended in one purpose, one voice and one sacred space.

The circle is woven by the priest and bards, or by priest and priestess (see Chapter 1). The circle may also be consecrated with incense and water. An incense burner is carried around the circle and the smoke wafted over each person present. A bowl of water is then taken around the circle, each person being sprinkled with a few drops.

**Priestess:** Let us call now to the quarters, that our ancestors may know the old ways are not forgotten.

### Calling the Quarters

Calling the quarters is a part of many traditions, invoking different energies from each of the cardinal points. Representatives of different faiths are invited to call the quarters, each in their own way. The following are merely suggestions, firstly in the Druid tradition:

**East:** I call to the spirits of air, the breath of life; to the spirit of the eagle who brings the gift of vision far and clear, the spirits of the wild east wind, of sunrise and of spring, of new life and new growth. May all within this circle know the power of your blessings. So I bid you hail and welcome!

**All:** Hail and welcome!

**South:** I call to the spirits of fire, of energy of passion; the spirit of the wild cat, who kindles within us the strength and beauty of the untamed places; spirit of the noonday sun, the heat of summer, vitality and abundance. May all within this circle know the power of your blessings. So I bid you hail and welcome!

**All:** Hail and welcome!

**West:** I call to the spirits of water, of the ebb and flow of emotion; to the spirit of the salmon, who fills us with the wisdom welling up from deep within the earth, of open seas and running streams, of cleansing rain; spirit of the evening sun, of twilight and of autumn. May all within this circle know the power of your blessings. So I bid you hail and welcome!

**All:** Hail and welcome!

**North:** I call to the spirits of earth, of the womb of creation; to the spirit of the bear, who draws us into the nourishing darkness of the cave; spirits of the night and the snows of winter, deep roots and ancient stones. May all within this circle know the power of your blessings. So I bid you hail and welcome!

**All:** Hail and welcome!

To follow are some suggestions from other traditions:

### East [Christian]:

> *The eye of the great God,*
> *The eye of the God of glory,*
> *The eye of the King of hosts,*
> *The eye of the King of the living,*
> *Pouring upon us*
> *At each time and season,*
> *Pouring upon us gently and generously.*
> *Glory to thee*
> *Thou glorious sun,*
> *Glory to thee, thou sun,*
> *Face of the God of life.*

### South [Shamanic]:

> *You, O Fire,*
> *Our mother with thirty teeth.*
> *You ride a red mare of three springs,*
> *Your red cloak flying in the wind.*
> *Through your garments run chains of mountains.*

In your veins the rivers flow.
Provide for us by day
And protect us by night.
Light the way for those who depart
And lead the others homeward.
O Fire, Great Mother, be with us.

## West [Wiccan]:

Ye Lords of the Watchtowers of the West,
ye Lords of Water,
ye Lords of Death and of Initiation;
I do summon, stir and call you up,
to witness our rites and to guard the Circle.

## North [Norse]:

Hail to Woden, wisest of Gods,
Howls of wolves and ravens' cries,
Be sig-runes writ on this bright day.
Hail to Freya, fiery love-queen,
Witch-wife, healer, warrior of trance.
Hail to the Gods and Goddesses all,
Hail the ancient ones,
Spirits most wise.

## Priest:

The circle is unbroken,
The ancestors awoken.
May the songs of the Earth
and of her people ring true.
Hail to the spirits of this place;
of root and branch, tooth and claw,
fur and feather, of earth and sea and sky.
Hail and welcome!

**All:** Hail and welcome!

## Handfasting

Handfasting is a traditional form of marriage once common in parts of Britain and treated as binding by the couple themselves, their families and communities.

**Priestess:** At sacred times and places such as this our ancestors clasped hands when they would wed, and such Handfastings were lawful, true and binding, for as long as love should last. Would any couple who would wish to make such vows, or to reaffirm existing vows, witnessed by this gathering, now come forward.

The couple requiring handfasting join hands.

**Priestess:** As the sun and moon bring light to the Earth, do you [name] and [name] vow to bring the light of love and joy to your union?
**Both:** I do.
**Priestess:** And do you vow to honour each other as you honour that which you hold most sacred?
**Both:** I do.
**Priestess:** And do you vow to maintain these vows in freedom, for as long as love shall last?
**Both:** I do.
**Priest:** Then let the Earth bear witness that [name] and [name] are joined in love and joy and freedom. So let it be!
**All:** So let it be!

The couple are then encouraged to exchange personal vows, either privately or so that all may hear, after which the assembly may say again: 'So let it be!' to signify that they have witnessed these vows. They may also exchange rings and/or blessings, love tokens, and so on sealing their bond with a kiss.

**Priest:** Let all bear witness that [name] and [name] are joined in love. May their love partake of the beauty, majesty and power of the sacred land, and may they grow together in wisdom, joy and harmony. My own blessing, and the blessings of all those assembled here be with you.

**Priestess:** The blessings of the Gods be with you.

**Priest:** The blessing of the Ancestors be with you.

**Priestess:** And with all that flows from your union.

**Priest:** So may it be!

**All:** So may it be!

## *Blessing for Children*

**Priestess:** Our circle is a symbol of the eternal, and yet it is made anew each time we meet. And so it is with ourselves; we each hold within us a spirit that is eternal, and yet we are reborn many times as we journey towards the centre. And at each moment of rebirth we are touched by the eternal spirit that guides us on our journey. Let the children who would be blessed come forward, creating a circle within the circle of our community.

Babies and young children may now come forward, with or without parents. Each child is given a blessing by the priestess. If there are many children to be blessed, it may be opportune to open the first eisteddfod session while this is being done. This is coordinated by the priest who invites members of the assembly to come forward with appropriate stories, poems and songs.

**Priestess:**

> *I baptise thee with Mother Earth,*
> *From whose loins we come*
> *And to whose arms we fly*
> *When our journey here is over.*
>
> *I baptise thee with the winds*
> *That come from the four corners*
> *Of the Earth, the winds that*
> *Scatter the seeds of the harvest*
> *And blow away the snows of winter.*
>
> *I baptise thee with fire*
> *So that thy spirit may be*
> *Purified and thy days*
> *Be long and fruitful.*
>
> *I baptise thee with the waters*
> *Of life, the waters that*
> *No living thing can do without.*
> *Give thanks to our Lady*
> *For thy bounteous harvest,*
> *And may she bless you and keep you*
> *All the days of your life.*

**Priestess:** Within the Gorsedd circle is the circle of our children, blessed by the Gods, blessed by our Mother Earth and by the elements of Earth, Water, Fire and Air. Let us welcome them into our community of spirit and of song. Children of our Mother Earth, I bid you hail and welcome!

**All:** Hail and welcome!

## Bardic Initiation

This simple form of initiation offers an opportunity to make a commitment to the bardic path and to the spirit of the place.

**Priestess:** As we are born into the life of the body, so we may be born into the life of the spirit. Initiation into the Gorseddau seeded by the British Druid Order offers an opportunity to dedicate to the spirit of place, the community of bards and kindred of the spirit. It is free and open to all who wish to receive it, welcoming followers of all spiritual traditions within one circle. In offering this initiation, we ask that you make a personal commitment to walk the path of the bard in beauty and in peace, using what inspiration you may gain to find your own spirit's true path of creative expression, and using your creativity for the benefit of your community and of the Earth.

**Priest:** Let those who wish to be initiated into the Gorsedd of Bards of [name of place] and to receive the spirit of inspiration that we call Awen, the flowing spirit, step forward now to the centre of the circle.

The candidates for initiation gather at the centre of the circle, linking hands to form an outward-facing circle of their own. All then repeat the following after the priest and priestess:

*We assemble here at* [name of festival] *of the year* [. . .].
*We assemble in the face of the sun; the Eye of Enlightenment.*
*We assemble on the Gorsedd mound of Mother Earth.*
*We assemble here to constitute ourselves a Gorsedd of Bards of the Isles of Britain.*

**Priest:** In the name of the ancient Order of Bards, and by the authority of those here present, I hereby proclaim this Gorsedd of [name of place]; may it be a meeting place of Love, and Truth, and Light. So let it be!

**All:** So let it be!

**Priestess:** Let us now invoke the Awen, the holy flowing spirit of the bardic tradition, and direct its shining stream of inspiration towards those gathered in the midst of the circle, that they may receive its glowing gifts of clear sight, wisdom and strength of spirit. And let those in the centre join the chant, visualising the stream of inspiration flowing into you, and through you, to energise and inspire not only yourselves, but the land of [name of place] and all the worlds beyond.

Those in the outer circle link hands. Those who have already received the Awen visualise its stream of inspiration flowing into the circle, directed through them to those gathered in the centre.

**All:** Awen, Awen, Awen.

Those in the outer circle then give the following blessing:

> *Wisdom of serpent be thine,*
> *Wisdom of raven be thine,*
> *Wisdom of valiant eagle.*
>
> *Voice of swan be thine,*
> *Voice of honey be thine,*
> *Voice of the son of stars.*
>
> *Bounty of sea be thine,*
> *Bounty of land be thine,*
> *Bounty of the boundless heavens.*

**Priest:** Step forward now, Bards of the Gorsedd of [name of place], and take your place within the circle of initiates.

All now return to their places in the circle.

**Priest:** Let us now proclaim the Gorsedd Prayer.

**All:**

> *Grant, O God and Goddess, thy protection,*
> *And in protection, strength,*
> *And in strength, understanding,*
> *And in understanding, knowledge,*
> *And in knowledge, the knowledge of justice,*
> *And in the knowledge of justice, the love of it,*
> *And in that love, the love of all existences,*
> *And in the love of all existences, the love of the*
> *God and Goddess and all goodness.*

**Priestess:** Everything the Power of the World does is done in a circle. The sky is round, and I have heard that the Earth is round like a ball, and so are all the stars. The wind in its greatest power whirls, and birds make their nests in circles, for theirs is the same religion as ours. The junction of heaven and earth, the horizon, is its circle of enclosing stones, for it is beyond the air that heaven and earth meet, and that junction is the circle of enclosing stones. Let us then complete our circle by joining hands to swear the oath of Peace.

All join hands and repeat the following three times:

**All:**

> *We swear by peace and love to stand,*
> *Heart to heart and hand in hand,*
> *Mark, O Spirit, and hear us now,*
> *Confirming this our sacred vow.*

## Honouring the Departed

**Priest:** The Otherworld is known by many names. Some call it the Islands of the Earthly Paradise, or the Isles of the Blest. These islands lie beyond the western ocean, where the souls of the departed are carried on the rays of the setting sun to the place of peace and healing.

**Priestess:** Those among us who have friends or loved ones who have taken or are about to take that journey are invited to speak their names, either aloud or in your hearts, that we may honour them.

Those who wish to may say the name or names aloud. Others may make their dedications in silence. A bard may sing a song or play a melody in honour of the departed and for the strengthening of those they leave behind.

**Priestess:** We give thanks, in the name of our Gods, for all those who have shared with us their lives, their wisdom and their love. Hail, O ancestors, those newly departed and those of old.
**All:** Hail, O ancestors!

## The Sharing

Priest and priestess bless the bread and mead.

**Priest:** We gather here today to celebrate [name of festival], the festival of [say what the festival is about].
**Priestess:** Let us now give thanks to our Mother Earth, from whom we all were born, and to whom we shall return at the end of our days.

The bread and mead are brought into the centre of the circle to be blessed by the priest and priestess.

**Priestess:** Mother Earth, in the name of our Gods and the Gods of our ancestors, we give you thanks. You nourish us body and soul with your gifts of beauty and of abundance. As you honour us with such precious life, may we honour you. I bless this bread in the name of [whatever spirits or deities may be deemed appropriate].

**Priestess:** This bread is blessed. To our Mother we give the first. I leave corn and milk in your land, and mast in your woods, and increase in your soil.

She breaks the bread and scatters some over the earth.

**Priest:** Father Sky, in the name of our Gods and the Gods of our ancestors, we give you thanks. Light of the sun and blessings of rain fall upon the body of our Mother, bringing forth her gifts. To you, O Father, we give thanks. I bless this mead in the name of [whatever spirits or deities may be deemed appropriate].

**Priest:** This mead is blessed. To you, our Mother, we give the first. I leave corn and milk in your land, and mast in your woods, and increase in your soil.

He pours some on the earth.

**Priestess:** Let us eat, that none may know hunger.
**Priest:** Let us drink, that none may know thirst.

Priest and priestess give the offerings to each other. With the help of the assisting priest and priestess, the bread and mead is shared with the gathering, passing sunwise around the circle. While the feast is shared, the eisteddfod begins.

**Priest:** As we give thanks for the gifts of food and drink that sustain our bodies, so let us give thanks in poetry and song for the gift of inspiration that uplifts our spirits.

Bards of the Gorsedd are now invited to give offerings of poetry, story or song in honour of the season, of the Earth and of the community. When the eisteddfod ends, the circle is closed as follows:

**Priestess:** I call upon the guardians of the quarters to close this Gorsedd circle.

**North:** Spirits of the North; spirits of earth, we give thanks for the gifts of strength and endurance that you have brought to our circle. May these gifts remain with us as we prepare to depart this place, and as we bid you hail and farewell!

**All:** Hail and farewell!

**West:** Spirits of the West; spirits of water, we give thanks for the gifts of deep wisdom and free flowing that you have brought to our circle. May these gifts remain with us as we prepare to depart this place, and as we bid you hail and farewell!

**All:** Hail and farewell!

**South:** Spirits of the South; spirits of fire, we give thanks for the gifts of passion and energy that you have brought to our circle. May these gifts remain with us as we prepare to depart this place, and as we bid you hail and farewell!

**All:** Hail and farewell!

**East:** Spirits of the East; spirits of air, we give thanks for the gifts of clarity and far sight that you have brought to our circle. May these gifts remain with us as we prepare to depart this place, and as we bid you hail and farewell!

**All:** Hail and farewell!

**Guardian:** I give thanks to all those, both seen and unseen, who have gathered here today. May all be blessed.

**Priestess:** O Spirit of this Place, we give you thanks for your blessings. Hail, O ancestors, O great Gods of old, we give you thanks for your presence, your guidance and your inspiration. May these gifts remain with us as we bid you hail and farewell!

**All:** Hail and farewell!

**Priestess:** Let the circle be opened that these blessings be shared throughout the world.

The Priest and three bards unweave the circle.

**Priest:** This rite ends in peace as in peace it began. May the spirit of [name of place], the light of sun and moon, the blessings of our ancestor and the power of the old gods go with us all to nourish, strengthen and sustain us as we depart this place. Peace without and peace within, until we meet again. So may it be!

**All:** So may it be!

Here ends this Gorsedd rite.

This portmanteau rite incorporates many elements of our tradition. It is an open, public representation of Druid practice, offering an opportunity for rites of passage to be witnessed and acknowledged by a broad community. Many find their spiritual needs well met by such open rites; others wish for individual rites of passage to be tailored more to their own needs and to be more private. A Druid priest will respond appropriately by working closely with those requiring the rite to ensure that their needs are fully met.

The rite given here is fairly complex. Most ritual within Druidry is simple, consisting of the few words we might say when we light a candle of blessing for a friend, greet our ancestors before our altar, pray for guidance for a loved one in need, or honour the spirit of a tree in a forest glade. These things have no written text. Like all the best rituals, they are spoken from the heart.

# 8

# Change

In this final chapter you may have most need of the concept of catmas (see Introduction). If you have forgotten what it was, I suggest that you go back and look at it now.

The Druid is a walker between the worlds. We have taken steps along that path in previous chapters, and have journeyed in imagination and in spirit. To become a Druid in the sense in which I understand it, we must go to the threshold between life and death, between this world and the worlds beyond, and step over it into new realms of consciousness.

A myth common to many traditional cultures tells of a Golden Age when those who walked between the worlds did so in body rather than in spirit. This Golden Age is looked upon as a remote mythical past, when humans talked freely with all other creatures and when the gods lived permanently in this world. The myth describes how humankind became divorced from the gods and the rest of the natural world, usually through some monumental act of human arrogance or stupidity. Then the gods withdrew into the Otherworld and people lost the ability to speak with animals. The spirit world was hidden from humankind. The role of the Siberian *shaman*, the Icelandic *seidkana*, the Lakota *wichasa wakan*, the Yaqui *brujo*, or the European Druid is to re-establish communication between the worlds, to move between them and bring back messages from ancestors, gods and spirits.

In most traditional cultures, illness or injury are believed to result from harm done to the sick person's spirit. Sometimes a part of the spirit becomes lost, detached or stolen; sometimes the whole spirit is lost or taken. The job of those who walk between the worlds is then to journey in the Otherworld, search out the missing soul-stuff and bring it back, restoring it to the person and, in the process, curing them. Traditional cures often combine herbs, rituals, prayers, chants and other elements, but the recovery of the patient's soul-stuff is at the heart of the process. Healing has been an important part of native European religion for millennia, and there are Druids today who work healing in the manner described.

## Boundaries Between the Worlds

The role of walker between the worlds engenders a fascination with boundaries and doorways that has long been part of Druid tradition. Any boundary or doorway, whether in time or space, in this world or those beyond, is seen as a potential passage by which we may pass between worlds. Our recent ancestors made prayers or ritual gestures each time they left or entered a house, our more remote ancestors buried animals or people at the entrances to shrines or stone circles, their spirits becoming guardians of the threshold. We also recognise seasonal festivals as doorways between the worlds, just as they are doorways taking us from one part of the year to another, from spring into summer, autumn into winter. Hallowe'en and May Eve in particular, but other festivals too, are seen as times when the souls of the dead mingle with the living, when the inhabitants of the Faery realm show themselves in wild dances beneath the moon. The twilight boundaries between day and night are also seen as peculiarly potent times to perform rituals or seek visions and inspiration. We recall these traditions when approaching a sacred grove or circle, when we pause at the gateway to honour, greet and be greeted by the spirit guardian of the place before we enter.

To be a walker between the worlds takes other forms besides spirit journeying; the Druid acts as a bridge-builder, promoting understanding and reconciliation between different cultures or interests; many Druids promote and take part in interfaith dialogues or work for peace between opposing factions through ritual, prayer or pilgrimage, or through more direct forms of mediation.

## Shape-Shifting

The Druid is also a shape-shifter. In the mythical Golden Age the power to shape-shift is said to have involved physically transforming the body from human to animal, bird, fish, reptile or insect. Nowadays such bodily transformations are rare and most shape-shifting occurs in spirit. Shape-shifting serves many purposes. For some, spirit transformation is part of the process by which they move between the worlds, using the senses, strength or speed of a particular animal in their Otherworld journeying.

What does it feel like to shape-shift? Strange. Some level of human consciousness usually remains in the background as an observer, but the main part, the part that senses the world, that makes decisions and acts on them, shifts into another state.

I was to take part in a ceremony at a Druid summer camp. It had been blisteringly hot for weeks and the ground was parched and tempers fraying. I decided that some rain-making was required but had not worked out how it would be done. As I approached the circle, I saw a silver bowl suspended above it from which silver liquid was falling on to the cracked earth. I knew this as a sign that I should abandon any conscious attempt to plan what I was to do, allowing the Awen to guide me. A little way into the ceremony I looked up into the cloudless sky and realised that to effect a change in the weather I needed to get up there. I had previously encountered a spirit eagle and began to dance the eagle's spirit dance, allowing my body to decide how to move. I whirled around, holding out my wolfskin cloak as wings, flapping them as I spun. The dance had the desired effect. My eagle helper came to me and our spirits merged. My human body was left behind and I rose swiftly into the air on power-ful wings. Looking down I saw the circle far below and my body still dancing. The eagle me began a parallel dance in the sky, circling rapidly. Soon I was joined by another three eagles coming in from the west. The four of us flew in circles, spiralling in towards the centre. As we did, fluffy white clouds appeared and moved towards us. They were followed by grey clouds, then thicker, darker clouds, until my cousins and I were flying in the raging heart of a thunder-storm, bolts of lightning coruscating around us, thrilling every cell with electrical energy. It was glorious!

When a bolt of lightning passed along the staff I held in my talons, I knew it was time to return to my human body. I bid farewell to my winged companions and swooped down to the circle. Finding my body, I slipped from the eagle's form and re-entered human consciousness. Having been whirling all that time, my body was so dizzy that I couldn't stand up.

Next day a brief, spectacular thunderstorm swept across the country in a line at the centre of which was our camp. On either side of us, twenty-three buildings were struck by lightning, though no one was injured. The land got the drenching it needed and the atmosphere of tension in the camp broke.

I once told this story to someone and their response was to pause for a moment, then say in a questioning tone: 'And you did this *without* taking drugs?' Absolutely. Except in some South American cultures, most traditional workers with spirit don't use drugs to shape-shift or make spirit journeys. In Siberia, where the term shaman originates, one who needs drugs to help him is considered a very poor shaman indeed.

Some time after that summer camp rite I read a novel called *The Way of Wyrd* by Brian Bates, in the first chapter of which the central character, a Saxon sorcerer, wears a wolf-skin cloak and performs a whirling dance, flapping his cloak while summoning the spirit of an eagle. I also found after the event that an old Welsh tradition maintains that storms are created by eagles who fly in the clouds around Mount Snowdon. The eagles who joined me above the circle that day came from the direction of Snowdonia and returned that way when they left.

## Dancing on the Edge

How do we develop the ability to shape-shift or to walk between the worlds? Usually not through choice. Often, such talents arise as a result of serious illness, either mental or physical, events that lead us to the edge of death, the gateway between this world and the world of the ancestors. On that edge, ancestral teachers or spirit guides, either human or animal, may appear, bringing the gift of healing and explaining how it may be given to others. Often, the recipient of these gifts is first plagued by persistent dreams or wild imaginings and turns to the spirit world to find how to cope with them. Often, they will be observed from early childhood to be Otherworldly, loners, day-dreamers. Some who possess these talents are willing to teach them to others. Teaching is another of the traditional roles of the Druid and there are those in the tradition today who run teaching groves or who take on apprentices who want to learn skills that can't adequately be conveyed in a book.

As with second sight, the shape-shifting and Otherworld journeying skills of the Druid are a double-edged sword. Working in a world of spirit that most people don't see or deny the existence of can tend to cut off those who take this path. And the things encountered in the spirit world are not always pleasant. Dealing with people who are sick in mind, body or spirit is difficult and demanding and once one has the skill it becomes very hard to turn away from it. To compensate for these difficulties, one finds assistance from ancestors, gods and guides, and from animal helpers. The latter are so prominent in traditional cultures all over the world that 'shamanism' has been called the way of the animal powers.

## Animal Powers

Power animals are individual spirit creatures who are strongly linked with us, spirit to spirit. They often act as guardians, guides and teachers, as well as sources of energy and inspiration. Sometimes a power animal will remain with you for life, or you may have a succession of power animals. Most people have one. To begin to work with it you first need to know what it is, and there are many ways you might find out. One is to go on a spirit journey with an experienced guide who will help you to find and meet your power animal. If this is not an option, you might look for an animal that crops up repeatedly in dreams or waking visions or that intrudes on your life in other ways. Or you might try meditation or divination within the sacred circle, preceded by an Awen chant.

Once you have discovered the identity of your power animal, you can begin to work with it by finding information about the animal, its habitat, food and behaviour. This will help you to form a relationship with the animal. You may find that a piece of fur, feather, skin or scale, tooth or claw will also help to bring you closer to your power animal. You may also create or hear in your head songs that will help you. In addition, play-acting your power animal can be very rewarding, perhaps making a mask or costume that represents it. As in the example of the eagle above, dancing your power animal is another potent way to connect with it. Once the initial connection is made, your own intuition, with the guidance of your power animal itself, should help you to build and maintain a good relationship with it. Such relationships can prove invaluable in pursuing the path of the Druid.

By no means all Druids develop the skills of shape-shifting, Otherworld journeying and soul healing, nor is it in any way necessary that they should. There are other, equally valuable areas in which to work. Teaching is a traditional Druidic role and one that can be intensely rewarding, as is the construction and performance of ritual. Counselling is another, peace-making another. Just as some artists work with paint, others with clay or steel, dance or music, so those who walk the path of Druidry find their own individual ways to express their inspiration, their connections with the sacred land and with our ancestors.

In this book I have tried to give a taste of contemporary Druidry. To capture any spiritual tradition on a printed page is not easy. I am aware even as I write that my words flow across the page like quicksilver, that meaning becomes elusive, sliding from the mind like water through the fingers. That is the way of Awen, the flowing spirit of the Druid tradition; it seldom remains still for long, always changing, flowing onward, its flow linking us spirit to spirit with our ancestors, with the changing tides of sun, moon and seasons, with the spirits of the land and the teachers of our tradition. Our task is to allow ourselves to flow and change with the Awen, riding its current like the Salmon of Wisdom in the legends of our ancestors, gaining fresh inspiration from each breath we take as we follow the rushing stream back to its source, the well-spring of the creative spirit. May your journey be blessed.

Hail and farewell!

# Useful Addresses

## Modern Druid Groups

An initial interest in Druidry is often followed by a desire to connect with others in the tradition. This is usually done by joining one or more of the many Druid groups that exist in Britain and around the world. These may offer training, companionship, celebration, ritual, networking, or offer all of these things. In the limited space available I have listed just a few, all of which offer good access to the Druid path.

*The British Druid Order*, PO Box 29, St Leonards-on-Sea, East Sussex, TN37 7YP, England.
The British Druid Order was founded in 1979 and is currently run by myself and joint chief Emma Restall Orr. It organises events, talks, workshops and rituals in Britain and around the world, including public and private rites of passage and celebrations of the eight festivals of the wheel of the year. It also has a growing network of local groves that offer ritual, companionship, celebration and training. The Order publishes books, magazines and other resources,

including the BDO journal, *Tooth & Claw*, and the magazine of Druidry ancient and modern, *The Druids' Voice*. The BDO website can be found at: http://www.druidorder. demon.co.uk

*The Gorsedd of Bards of the Isles of Britain*, c/o BDO, PO Box 29, St Leonards-on-Sea, East Sussex, TN37 7YP, England. The Gorsedd organises open, multifaith celebrations of the eight seasonal festivals at sacred sites both in Britain and overseas. Ceremonies are family events, held within the spirit of Druidry yet open to followers of all faiths and traditions, offering rites of passage, initiation into the Gorsedd and open eisteddfod. In America, contact: *The Gorsedd of Bards of Caer Pugetia*, PO Box 9785, Seattle, WA 98109, USA.

*The Order of Bards, Ovates and Druids*, PO Box 1333, Lewes, East Sussex, BN7 1DY.
The Order of Bards, Ovates and Druids is the largest Druid group worldwide, with seed groups and groves in many countries. It was founded by Ross Nichols in 1964, lapsed after his death in 1975, but was revived by current chosen chief, Philip Carr-Gomm, in 1988. It runs a correspondence course supported by tutors that provides a well-balanced, structured framework guiding students through the 'grades' of bard, ovate and Druid. The OBOD website can be found at: http://www.druidry.org

*The Henge of Keltria*, PO Box 48369, Minneapolis, MN 55448-0369, USA. The Henge of Keltria is one of the largest US-based Druid groups. It offers a correspondence course with a strong Celtic, particularly Irish, flavour. It has groves around the country.

There are many other Druid groups, far too many to list here. If you'd like to find out about some of the larger ones, the British Druid Order publishes the *Druid Directory*. Write enclosing an SAE for details.

## *World Wide Web*

There are tens of thousands of websites devoted to Druidry and all things Celtic. The three listed here are among the best and all provide good links to other resources.

British Druid Order: http://www.druidorder.demon.co.uk/
Order of Bards, Ovates and Druids: http://www.druidry.org/
IMBAS: http://www.imbas.org/

# Further Reading

There are probably more books in print about Druidry now than at any other time in history. I have, therefore, been very selective in those listed here.

## Contemporary Druidry

Philip Carr-Gomm, *Elements of the Druid Tradition*, Element Books, 1991. A good introduction to Druidic belief and practice, covering both the actual and mythical history of the tradition.

Philip Carr-Gomm, *The Druid Way*, Element Books, 1993. A sacred journey through the landscape of the South Downs, weaving the author's experience of Druidry with philosophy, history, ritual and folklore.

Philip Carr-Gomm (ed.), *The Druid Renaissance*, Thorsons, 1996. A wide-ranging collection of articles by many leading figures in modern Druidry.

Emma Restall Orr, *Principles of Druidry*, Thorsons, 1998. An excellent introduction to the broad spectrum of Druidic belief and practice.

Emma Restall Orr, *Spirits of the Sacred Grove*, Thorsons, 1998.

A deeply moving, personal account of the life and work of a Druid priestess through the eight festivals of the sacred year.

Emma Restall Orr, *Ritual: A Druid's Guide to Life, Love and Inspiration*, Thorsons, 2000

## Ancient Druidry

Peter Berresford Ellis, *The Druids*, Constable, 1994. A good survey of Druid history, rather dismissive of contemporary Druidry.

Miranda Green, *Exploring the World of the Druids*, Thames & Hudson, 1997. Very good on early history and medieval references, excellent illustrations, a little shaky on contemporary Druidry.

Ronald Hutton, *Pagan Religions of the Ancient British Isles*, Basil Blackwell, 1991. A superb survey of the spiritual life of Britain from the first inhabitants to the present day.

T. D. Kendrick, *The Druids,* Senate, 1996 (reprint of 1927 edition): very good survey of Druid history including translations of all the classical Greek and Roman references.

## The Ritual Year

Ronald Hutton, *Stations of the Sun*, Oxford University Press, 1996. A brilliant history of the ritual year in Britain.

## Bardic Tales

Jeffrey Gantz, *The Mabinogion*, Penguin Books, 1976. A sound modern translation of this great collection of Welsh legends.

Lady Gregory, *Gods and Fighting Men*, Colin Smythe, 1970. A poetic rendering of the Irish Book of Invasions and the legends of Finn mac Cool.

Thomas Kinsella, *The Tain*, Oxford University Press, 1970.

A poetic, powerful translation of the legends of Ulster's champion, Cuchulainn.

Philip Shallcrass, *The Story of Taliesin*, British Druid Order, 1997. Annotated translation of this seminal text.

## *Bardic Performance*

Greywolf (Philip Shallcrass), *The Sign of the Rose*, BDO, 1999. A CD featuring songs, chants and poetry inspired by and dedicated to the goddess in all her myriad forms.

Ronald Hutton, *The Mabinogion*, Talking Myth, 1997. Cassette readings of the four branches of *The Mabinogion* with musical accompaniment.

Robin Williamson, *Gems of Celtic Story One & Two*, Pig's Whisker Music (1998). *Gems One* features *The Mabinogion* tale of Culhwch and Olwen; *Two* features four Irish tales including the Birth of Lugh. For further information on Robin's CDs, tapes, books and tours, contact: Pig's Whisker Music, PO Box 114, Chesterfield, Derbyshire S40 3YU, England.

## *Divination*

Stephanie and Philip Carr-Gomm, *The Druid Animal Oracle*, Simon & Schuster, 1995. Superb illustrations by Bill Worthington make this one of the most beautiful divinatory card sets available.

Nigel Pennick, *The Secret Lore of Runes and Other Magical Alphabets*, Rider, 1991. Runes, Oghams, Coelbren and the rest.

Philip Shallcrass, *The Druid Tarot*, British Druid Order, 1994. A 25 card set based on original woodcuts from 3,000 years of European pagan iconography.

## Trees

Jaqueline Memory Paterson, *Tree Wisdom*, Thorsons, 1997.
Druidic tree lore.

## Animals

Gordon MacLellan, *Sacred Animals*, Capall Bann, 1997. An
inspiring book on working with spirit animals.
See also *The Druid Animal Oracle* ('Divination').

## Wyrd

Brian Bates, *The Wisdom of the Wyrd*, Rider, 1996. The world-
view of Anglo-Saxon sorcery made accessible for today.

# Index

**Index**